For Hows...

Gerda Davidson

10. xii. 83

ISLES OF HOME

Shetland

Isles of Home

Sixty Years of Shetland

Gordon Donaldson

Paul Harris Publishing

Edinburgh

First published 1983 by
Paul Harris Publishing
40 York Place
Edinburgh

ISBN 0 86228 069 9

Printed by The Shetland Times Ltd.
Prince Alfred Street, Lerwick
Shetland

Contents

Acknowledgements

My acknowledgements in this book are in the main not of the conventional type to those who helped in one way or another with the preparation of the text. My indebtedness in this case extends back over so many years to those friends in Shetland who contributed in so many ways to my happiness on my visits. I sometimes think of how much I took for granted, rather thoughtlessly, in early days, encouraged by Shetlanders' hospitality and generosity. One was so apt just to assume that one would always be welcome, that there would always be a meal, there would always be a bed and so on. I cannot help feeling now that such thanks as I did express at the time were hopelessly inadequate and I take this opportunity to make amends, but with the sad limitation that so many of those to whom I feel gratitude are no longer with us.

The great majority of the illustrations came from my own photographs and several (10, 30, 34, 35, 37, 38, 39, 59) from photographs taken by my late mother or father. It is a pleasure to express my thanks to others to whom I owe photographs, including: the J. D. Rattar Collection in the Shetland Library and Museum (23, 25). The Shetland Times Ltd. (19); R. Williamson (48); Mrs Ivy Jardine (11, 14); the late Miss Ann Moar (46); John Peterson (7). It is not easy to be certain of the origin of all the items in such a miscellaneous collection accumulated over so many years, and in at least one case (47) the name of the photographer is no longer known to me. But to all of those to whom I owe photographs, named or unnamed, known or unknown, my warm gratitude.

Gordon Donaldson

October, 1983

List of Illustrations

1 ⬛ *A Land of Change and Contrasts*

When I arrived in Lerwick on one of my recent visits it happened to be rather a dull morning. I ran over in my mind the various places I wanted to visit or re-visit and ruled out areas where I would be interested primarily in the scenery and would therefore want bright conditions and good visibility. After a little thought I decided to go over to the island of Bressay, where my objectives would be not to view scenery but to look at some medieval remains and to visit an old friend. So I left Lerwick, that hive of industry. The town had always had a busy waterfront, thronged with the fishing boats of many nations, but by the late 1970s it had all the activity connected with oil developments. These, apart from causing many additional shipping movements in the harbour, had already transformed its north mouth with massive new installations which quite obliterated the old landscape.

I took my car on to the new vehicle ferry, which whisks one over the sound in four or five minutes, and landed in Bressay. There I made for my first objective, the ruins of the old church at Cullingsbrough at the northeast corner of the island. I found myself in a quiet secluded bay, behind me a burn with remains of traditional Shetland mills, and before me the sea; there was no sound save the waves lapping on the shore and no sign of life save the eider ducks breasting the waves and the sheep cropping the grass. My immediate reaction was that the oil and everything connected with it might have been a million miles away. The same thought has recurred to me many times since as I have moved around the islands. It happened again just a few days after that visit to Bressay, when I was in a very similar place, the Wick of Gruting at the north-east corner of Fetlar. Despite the oil, nothing at all had changed in the scene since my last visit to that wick, nearly thirty years before, except that this time the sun was not shining.

Yet on that first morning, in Bressay, I did not reflect long before my thoughts turned to changes as well as to contrasts. I recalled the first visit I ever paid to Bressay, in 1922. At the sea-front of Lerwick the little boy, fascinated by the small boats and by the launch which was ready to leave the old Bressay slip at Victoria Pier and cross the sound, prevailed on his mother to go aboard. We reached Bressay and had a walk around, then came back to the pier, only to find that the last ferry-boat for the day had left. It seemed a disaster, and it was brought home to me in no uncertain terms that it was all my fault, because it had been my idea to make the trip. I was reduced to tears, to be told, brutally but accurately, 'Crying won't help'. Fortunately we found a man who happened to be crossing to Lerwick in his own motor-boat, and he was kind enough to take us with him. Perhaps it was a salutary introduction to the hazards of visiting islands and depending on other people's boats rather than having a boat of one's own, but at any rate that recollection of the casual conditions of earlier times provided a sufficiently pointed contrast to the efficiency of the regular ferry service across Bressay Sound in the late 1970s.

And when I was on that beach at Cullingsbrough beside the ruined church I looked north to the Hoo Stack, the Mull of Eswick and on to Whalsay, out over the waters which used to be the sailing track of the North Isles steamer on which I had made so many trips during more than half a century. Here again was change, for I could not help recalling the old pattern of North Isles transport:

the *Earl of Zetland* (or rather two successive *Earls* which together served the islands for 98 years) going out the north mouth from Lerwick and making her calls at Whalsay, Burravoe, Mid Yell, Uyeasound, Hubie, Skerries and so many other ports where the ship had lain at anchor while goods and passengers, mail and cattle, were handled in flitboats. This was something I knew I had seen for the last time, because vehicle ferries had taken over stage by stage and the second *Earl* made her final trip in 1975.

While ferries had replaced the *Earl,* elsewhere bridges had replaced ferries. There had long been bridges to Muckle Roe, between the two largest islands in the Skerries group and between East and West Burra, but more recently bridges linked the Mainland to Trondra and Trondra to Burra.

My themes, then, are contrast and change. The 70s of the twentieth century will very likely go down in history as the era of the greatest revolution which ever took place in Shetland's economy and society, as a result of the exploitation of the oil discovered under the bed of the North Sea east of Shetland and the creation of the massive oil base at Sullom Voe, a place which had hardly been heard of before. Even now some BBC announcers and high civil servants have not yet learned to pronounce the name correctly. And, despite the enormous publicity given to Sullom Voe, there is still appalling ignorance about even the geographical position of the islands — owing partly to the reluctance of cartographers to place them properly on their maps or even to show them at all. A couple of years ago in Lerwick I met a hitch-hiker who had boarded the *St Clair* at Aberdeen under the impression that the voyage he was beginning at 6 p.m. would end at 8 p.m. and not at 8 o'clock next morning. If Sullom Voe was known at all before the oil era it was because it led up to the Mavis Grind, that remarkable isthmus where little more than the breadth of a road

separates the North Sea from the Atlantic. That feature
apart, the surroundings of the voe consisted mainly of
somewhat desolate and bleak stretches, with few hills
rising from the moorland, and it was surely one of the
quietest and least disturbed of all stretches of water. The
changes have been enormous, not only in the physical
appearance of the voe itself but in the economy of its
hinterland, which may be said to comprise the whole of
Shetland. The ramifications have affected the whole
group of islands, and the labour force in the construction
phase at Sullom Voe drew heavily not only on the
Mainland but on Yell, from which, thanks to the regular
ferries, men and women could travel to work each day.

A change hardly less spectacular than that at Sullom
Voe had come about a few years earlier as a result of
Shetland's place in the N.A.T.O. defence structure and
the construction of a huge radar station on the summit of
Unst's highest hill — R.A.F. Saxavord. The Sullom Voe
installations are massive, but they are mostly at shore
level, except for the two lofty stacks where the surplus gas
is flared off, whereas the Saxavord structure sits on a hill
928 feet high. Besides, Saxavord, at the extreme north-
east of Shetland, is the first thing a navigator may
recognise when he makes his landfall after crossing the
North Sea from Norway. In 1969, approaching Shetland
from the north-east after crossing from Aalesund, I
observed three 'pimples' on the horizon, one of them
immediately identifiable as Saxavord from the excre-
scence on its summit; the others, I judged, were the Vord
Hill of Fetlar and Roeness Hill.

Yet, without minimising the changes of the 1970s, it
is worth while looking farther back and reminding
ourselves of earlier changes which are now receding into
history. The half-century before the oil era — probably
like many another half-century over the ages — had seen
changes which were less spectacular and more gradual
but which cumulatively amounted to vast alterations in

what would previously have been thought of as the traditional Shetland way of life. The biggest change in my lifetime was the decline and, finally, the collapse of the herring fishing, which was so actively pursued in the fifty years down to the 1930s, not only in Lerwick but throughout the islands. In the peak year of 1905 there were no less than 174 'stations' where herring were landed, gutted and barrelled, 46 of them in Baltasound, 36 in Lerwick and others in about 30 more places. By the later 1930s there were hardly any outside Lerwick, and now scarcely a trace is to be seen of all the structures connected with that vast activity. Equally hard to detect are the remains of the installations connected with another enterprise, the whaling which was pursued at Roeness Voe, Collafirth and Olnafirth from 1903 to 1928. There have been later changes in the pattern of fishing — the exploitation of lobsters, crabs and scallops, the shipping of frozen fish direct to America, the erection of fish-processing factories — and one wonders what traces they will leave for the archaeologists of the future, who may well devise curious theories to explain the phenomenal middens created by the refuse from the processing factories. The latest device to reap a fresh harvest from the sea is the mooring of mussel-rafts, on the ropes attached to which mussels are expected to multiply.

These were conspicuous changes, but others, though more subtle, had been so profound that some of the conditions and the way of life which I recall from the 1920s and 1930s now seem almost as remote as the middle ages. Many of my recollections are no doubt quite trivial, but as an historian I am very conscious of the gaps in our knowledge of earlier periods which exist simply because people in the past did not put down on paper everyday happenings in the way I propose to do. Many have a far better right than I have to offer a picture of half a century of Shetland life and could do so with fuller knowledge.

But have they done so? And if no one were to do so, future historians would be so much the poorer.

My own acquaintance with Shetland now extends over nearly the whole of a fairly long life, and I have been an assiduous visitor to the islands since 1921, when, as a very small boy, I first set foot on Victoria Pier. I was born in Edinburgh, and even my father was born in Edinburgh, so I must go back to my grandfather for a native Shetland ancestor. But my father had been a regular visitor to the islands throughout his life — ever since, so he told me, his uncle Willie took him there for a holiday when he was only three. That would be in 1881, and they travelled north on the paddle *St Magnus* and landed at Lerwick by a flitboat before Victoria Pier was built. People sometimes say to me, 'But Donaldson is not a Shetland name'. True, it is not now, and the name is all but extinct, for my numerous cousins (in varying degrees) in the islands are all through females, but in the eighteenth century Yell and Fetlar seem to have been stuffed with Donaldsons, as the Parish Registers show. My father, like my great-grandfather, was Magnus, and he had two first cousins who bore that historic northern Christian name. Because of my father's connection with Shetland I had already heard a good deal about the islands before I ever went there and had met cousins from Shetland who from time to time visited us in Edinburgh. Already some of the homely Shetland words and phrases were familiar to me, and although I have never acquired any facility in the dialect and especially in the remarkable subtleties of its vowel sounds, the foundation must have been laid in my earliest childhood of the readiness with which I turn to an expressive Shetland word or idiom. In a total of sixty-three visits, up to 1983, all carefully recorded, I reckon I have spent in the aggregate 987 days in the islands, which (approaching three years) might almost be said to constitute a residential qualification. It has been one of the most satisfying experiences of my life to be accepted as a member of that island community, and wherever else I have gone my thoughts have never been far from those islands which the inhabitants, in their kindly and hospitable way, have so long allowed me to regard as 'home'.

I paid two visits with my father in 1921 and 1922, on the second occasion with my mother as well (making her first visit). I was not in Shetland again until 1929, when I was able to go on my own, and it was on that visit that I in effect discovered the place for myself and began my long love-affair with it. I suppose that at the age of eight or nine I had been too immature to appreciate either the scenic beauty of the islands or the historico-romantic flavour of the northern world. Both of those struck me very forcibly at the age of sixteen. Possibly the gap of seven years between my second visit and my third was an advantage, for the beginning of the love-affair might have been less passionate had it been more gradual.

Not a great deal remains in my mind from the visits in 1921 and 1922. There were the features which had a striking element of novelty, beginning with the voyage north, which was something of an adventure for a boy of eight. My father had a liking for the indirect boat, via Kirkwall, and a favourite ship for him, as for many more, was 'the steady old *St Rognvald*' — second of the name — on which he had travelled on her maiden voyage in 1901. I remember quite vividly going aboard that vessel at Leith on a Thursday evening for a sailing at midnight and having a very slow voyage, as there was a coal-strike that year and speeds were cut to economise fuel. I kept a diary, but of course it disappeared long ago. I remember that it began: 'Left Leith midnight. Arrived Aberdeen 10.15 a.m.' Perhaps I made no more entries. There seemed to be the better part of a day in Aberdeen and the better part of a day in Kirkwall, and, which was even more exciting, some hours by night in Kirkwall on the way south. It was my introduction to Aberdeen, with its

Marischal College, and to Kirkwall, with its Cathedral which I have so often visited since and of which I never grow weary, as well as its Bishop's and Earl's Palaces. Then the arrival in Lerwick, with our cousins to welcome us on the pier, as they always did. It was many, many visits later that I remarked that it was the first time I landed on the pier without being greeted by my cousin Jimmie. (Perhaps one should add that until the Second World War the ships generally arrived in the height of the day or in the afternoon and not at daybreak, so there was more likely to be a reception party.) We spent a few days in Lerwick, where we climbed to the top of the Town Hall tower and went out to the Clickimin, Sound and Gulberwick.

But the real objective was Yell, which I knew well enough as the ancestral home. From Lerwick to Burravoe meant then the old *Earl of Zetland,* already forty-four years old, and while other ships — the south boats — were to come and go in my experience over the next quarter of a century, the *Earl* remained the permanent feature. I remember, even from those distant days of 1921, a leisurely voyage by Whalsay, Skerries and Hubie, then the arrival at Burravoe, landing at the Brough pier from the flitboat, with the Aald Haa dominating the scene as it had done for centuries and still does. And Aunt Martha (my father's aunt) at the pier to welcome us and help to carry our luggage the two-and-a-half miles to Hamnavoe.

Yell, of course, had far more novelties for me than Lerwick, and my first acquaintance with those novelties is still constant in my memory. Lerwick was after all a town, with material comforts very much as one had in Edinburgh, including a water supply in the house. The one novelty in Lerwick was that the water which issued from the tap in those days was so peaty as to be of the colour of whisky; adequate filtering and treatment did not come until 1931. The country had different standards altogether, then and for long after. Perhaps the peat fire and open hearth and the methods of cooking — the very core of family life — intrigued me most. I remember my first sight of the big pot or kettle hanging on a chain down the lum — something still to be seen in some houses, but now very rarely indeed — and the technique of breaking down a piece of glowing peat on the hearth to cook food in a frying pan or to keep the teapot hot. And, years afterwards, whenever I caught an unexpected whiff of the kindly smell of the peat reek, as I often did in the West Highlands, the vision it immediately summoned up in my mind was of Martha stooping low over the hearth as she made tea. It was no doubt true then, as it long continued to be, that the diet consisted largely of fish, eggs, milk and mutton and that little except tea, sugar and bacon was bought from the shop two and a half miles away, but the healthy appetite of a small boy had no quarrel with a restricted, but ample, menu. I carried away a clear impression of domestic industry — the carding and the spinning, the incessant knitting, with Martha using a bunch of feathers stuck in her belt to take the thrust of the end of a knitting needle (a practice she never abandoned, though others adopted a belt with a pad incorporated in it). I was not offended by the lack of running water and facilities for baths and sanitation, because I had encountered such conditions in the country in mainland Scotland; indeed, the way we used to survive almost suggests that modern fads about hygiene are exaggerated. The dip well, however, was something new, and I made my acquaintance with the clear and ample spring water of the well in Lower Hamnavoe, from which I was to carry many a pail over the next fifty years or so. The large flat stone covering it, with its circular aperture for lowering a pitcher through, had been fashioned, so I was told, by my great-grandfather, who was indeed designated a stone-mason. One always had to take a pitcher, from which the full-sized pail was filled, and in later years I was faintly irritated by the usual practice of carrying back only the

B

single pail with the pitcher instead of filling a second pail and so saving a journey.

There were outdoor activities for a small boy, in the company of my father and his cousin, the late Magnie Donaldson. The Hamnavoe Burn was only a few hundred yards from the house. My father was much addicted to 'the trout burn', but angling in a burn was never to appeal much to me. However, from time to time when it was a novelty I dangled a rod in the Grey Stane Hole, a few yards upstream from the carefully laid stepping-stones which my great-uncle had put together for access to his peats and which were known as 'Willam Denelson's brig'. For years a stroll out through the Coo Grind at the end of the track past the houses of Lower Hamnavoe and across to the familiar burn was always my first outing when I arrived. A greater novelty in 1921 was a trip to Orfasay, the first of innumerable visits to that little island. It was the first boating expedition anywhere that sticks firmly in my mind, but there were plenty of other novelties that day beyond the mere fact of being afloat. It was the first time — the first of countless times — that I landed on an uninhabited island, the first time I was afloat alongside rocks, where Magnie put his hand down into the water to bring up a sea-urchin from its rocky attachment. Magnie had a gun and had shots at two seals. No doubt that was an exciting novelty too, for I was not then too humanitarian to approve of seal-hunting. In later years, when I had a boat of my own, I was to go to some lengths of deviousness to avoid being a party to the killing of creatures which I have never been able to look on with any feeling other than affection.

Those early visits in 1921 and 1922, while they certainly left abiding impressions on my memory, may be said to represent a kind of twilight zone before I emerged into the light of day with my first adult, or at any rate adolescent, visit in 1929.

The gap of seven years between 1922 and 1929

enabled me to notice changes which had taken place even then. For one thing, whereas in 1922 all the women were spinning, in 1929 no one — at any rate no one I saw — was spinning, at least as a normal activity. The wool was going to the mills for spinning. Knitting had taken on a new character. The 'Fair Isle' patterns, although they had been traditional in the islands, as they or something like them had been in all the northern countries, had become all the rage, and the busy fingers of Shetland women turned from their shawls or 'haps' and their spencers to Fair Isle pullovers, in both natural and dyed colours and with the pattern not merely in borders but 'all-over'. Houses, too, were changing. There were now far fewer thatched roofs, which I think probably passed from being in a majority to being in a minority in the 'twenties. Many crofters had taken advantage of grants or loans which enabled them not only to put on a tarred roof or one of asbestos slates but to raise the walls and add a modest attic storey. There were changes indoors as well. Open fires, like thatched roofs, were now in a minority, their places taken by black stoves, which the conservative denounced as so much less 'lightsome' — to which the obvious retort was that anyone who wanted the cheer of an open fire could go and sit 'ben', for the stove was of course in the 'but' or kitchen end of the house. The stoves revolutionised the diet, which became so much more varied. Four or more pots and pans could sit on the stove, and there was an oven in which it was possible to roast a piece of succulent lamb, the tender flesh of which melted in the mouth. The gridiron, which had previously been placed over hot peats broken down on the hearth, could still be used, now on top of the stove, so that the housewife could continue to turn out those delightful wavy 'bannocks'. Lighting as well as heating had changed in the 1920s. A single-wick paraffin lamp had, before my time, superseded the ancient 'collie' (which I never saw in use), but by 1929 even the improved paraffin

lamp with a circular wick and a mantle was being in turn
superseded by the pressure-lamp which remained
standard until electricity displaced it more than a
generation later.

The changes between 1922 and 1929 stand out in my
memory. There may have been equally significant
changes in the 1930s, and I certainly noted the arrival of
the telephone in the North Isles in 1936-7 and the spread
of the wireless set, which was extremely rare in 1929 but
almost universal a decade later. Yet the 'thirties seem in
retrospect a period almost of standstill, and some changes
probably failed to register on me, because I was in
Shetland so much then. In my last two years at school
(1929-31) and during my years as a student, first at
Edinburgh (1931-5) and then at London (1935-8),
Shetland was my main, almost my only, holiday place. I
spent nearly the whole of the long vacations there, and
also paid visits in the Easter and Christmas vacations. My
record year was 1934, when I spent the whole of July,
August and September in Shetland. There were other
years in which I had two or two-and-a-half months there,
but the three months of 1934 seem to have left a
particularly strong impression. When I recall various
incidents and then track them down it often turns out that
they took place in that wonderful year. The longer I
stayed the harder it was to wrench myself away, and I was
always in tears when I left, especially as I made the round
of farewells in Lower Hamnavoe and Aunt Martha would
say, 'Gude grant that on earth or in heaven we shall a'
meet again'. In one of those years of a long holiday —
surely it was 1934 — I must have carried the marks of
grief on my countenance even when I was on the south
boat between Lerwick and Aberdeen, for Mrs Pritchard
Williams, wife of the minister of Sandsting, remarked to
me on the *St Sunniva,* 'I never saw anybody so broken-
hearted at leaving Shetland'. To some extent those years
of long holidays as a student created for me a kind of

norm: Shetland in the 1930s. I measure things as happening before and after that phase. The 'twenties are rather remote and less well remembered, the period since the Second World War has passed with apparent rapidity, and I feel, as most of my generation do, that the world has never again been as pleasant a place as it was before 1939. The thirties. 'These were the days', as a Shetland contemporary of mine once remarked when we were reminiscing.

The long holidays of early days became a thing of the past. In 1938 I joined the staff of the Register House, which meant that I had only office leave, then came the War, to disrupt our old habits. I was not in Shetland in the years 1940-44, but resumed my visits in 1945. In 1947 I became a lecturer in the University, but this did not mean a return to vacations free from work and care in the manner of undergraduates. There was no question of reverting to the old practice of clearing off to Shetland for two or three months in the summer. I did, at the same time, see that I need not remain constantly in Edinburgh during the vacations and therefore set about looking for a second house somewhere in the country. I did seriously consider looking for one in Shetland, which had so many attractions — the many, many friends I had there, the physical familiarity of areas where I knew every stone in the hill and every rock in the sea, and — what is even more precious — that intangible sense of really belonging to the place. But I decided reluctantly that it would not have been practicable, or at any rate not sensible. I could not have gone to Shetland for weekends, and, equally, once there I could not have nipped down to Edinburgh for a day or for a few hours when the need arose. I turned my attention to Argyll, parts of which I had explored during the war years, and eventually acquired a cottage in the Benderloch district, where I was warmly welcomed and made many friends. It had comparative convenience of access by road and in those days there was still a

reasonable train service; it had superb scenery; and it had
the sea. I imported a certain element of Shetland into it,
because I acquired a Shetland boat and a Shetland tuskar
and spade to cut my peats on my own ground. Despite the
discouragement of rain and tempests, I kept my Benderloch house — or rather two successive houses, for in 1964
I had a new one built — for sixteen years, and finally gave
it up when commitments in Edinburgh seemed constantly
to multiply and it became increasingly trying to hammer
back and forward on that 125-mile road.

With commitments in Edinburgh, the Benderloch
house and a certain amount of travel abroad — beginning, belatedly but significantly, with a visit to Iceland
in 1950 — I never again after the war had as long holidays
in Shetland as I had had before 1939, though I once
achieved six weeks. My visits were mostly short,
sometimes very short indeed, but they became more
numerous. Once, for special reasons, I was in Shetland
four times in twelve months. In August 1969, when, only
ten days after the conclusion of the Historical Congress in
Lerwick over which I had the honour to preside, I was
back again in Lerwick, this time on a National Trust
Cruise, the Harbour-Master, the late Captain Inkster,
welcomed me at the Bressay slip with the words, 'You
might as well bide here a' the time'. In 1980, which was
the sixtieth year since my first visit in 1921, I made, so it
happened, my sixtieth visit. But although my Shetland
holidays were now shorter, they greatly extended my
knowledge of the islands, partly because I had more
money at my disposal. Already before 1939 I had been
from Sumburgh to Fethaland and Hermaness and had
stayed in Yell, Unst and Fetlar, besides visiting many
smaller islands, but after the war I added Whalsay,
Burra, Papa Stour, Skerries, Foula and Fair Isle to the
collection of inhabited islands on which I had landed.

A significant contribution to my travels was made by
National Trust Cruises, not so much the 'big-ship'

cruises on the *Uganda,* though they took me more than once to Lerwick and twice round Fair Isle, as by the May cruises on the *Regina Maris* under the command of Captain Alfred Vögel, a skipper who entered into the spirit of the thing and would go to almost any lengths to ensure that his passengers saw what the itinerary promised them. He once spent the better part of an afternoon dodging around Gigha trying (ultimately in vain) to find a position which gave enough lee to make it possible to send launches ashore with passengers. On a cruise which was to include three days in Shetland waters, in 1972, the schedule was Skerries, Fetlar, Unst, round the Flugga, Noss, Mousa and Fair Isle. Early on the first morning I saw the Noup of Noss through rising mist, and the sun broke through but with a stiff south-easterly breeze. We made for the north-east mouth at Skerries, the entrance generally used by the *Earl,* but of course the 6000-ton *Regina Maris* had to lie outside, and boat-work would have been impossible there that morning. We then moved round to the north mouth, where there was more shelter and the launches were able to carry us into the wonderful lagoon in the midst of those islands, which I had so often visited on the *Earl* and where I had once before been ashore for a couple of hours. At Fetlar in the afternoon we were due to land at Hubie, and Captain Vögel went in to a position which to passengers seemed perilously close to the rocks (but of course he had the advantage of a bow-thruster), only to find that landing at the pier, exposed to the south-east, was out of the question. He moved round to the other regular landing-place in Fetlar, Brough Lodge, but the sea sweeping up Colgrave Sound made that impracticable too. Not to be outdone, he went on to Oddsta (where the works had just begun for the terminal for the vehicle ferry), and managed to land us there. All the limited transport in Fetlar was mobilised to carry passengers to the hall at Leagarth, while others preferred to inspect the snowy owls which were then breeding in the island. Baltasound, in the evening, presented no problems. The programme, however, had been to lie there overnight and proceed in the morning round the Flugga, but this time we were defeated not by the weather but because — incredibly — the ship had run out of fresh water, and in the morning we woke to find ourselves tied up in Lerwick. I was especially disappointed because it was the second time my hope of getting round the Flugga had been dashed: in 1969 we had intended to wind up the Historical Congress with a grand cruise round the North Isles on the *Earl*, but the weather had caused us to abandon it. It is unlikely now that I shall ever go round the Flugga. However, the day on the *Regina Maris* which started, disappointingly, in Lerwick, turned out to be a success, for we landed on Noss in the afternoon, and in the evening visited Mousa, then lay overnight in Mousa Sound. Next day we were due to land on Fair Isle, but the wind was still too strong for that, and we ran on to Kirkwall instead. My landings on Fair Isle and Foula came on a single wonderful day in the course of a later *Regina Maris* cruise. After three days in Faroe during which we had persistent fog, the stewardess came in that morning to announce with evident surprise, 'Today the sun is shining', and we had excellent conditions for both the Shetland islands. Experiences on these cruises, while they amply demonstrate the hazards and unpredictability of such ventures, do illustrate the unequalled advantage which travel by sea offers for viewing Shetland. Unhappily the opportunities to view the islands in this way by public transport have now dwindled almost to extinction.

All my visits to Shetland in recent years have drawn to my notice changes great and small. Decline in the rural population — however much it may be offset by the continued expansion of Lerwick and concentration at various 'growth points' — is brought sharply to mind by the sight of houses where I used to be made welcome but

1 *St Sunniva* (II) arriving Leith 7th June, 1931

2 *St Sunniva* (II) on stocks at Aberdeen 1st April, 1931

3 *St Magnus* (IV), ex *St Clair* (II), at Leith

4   Arrival of second *Earl* at Lerwick 19th August, 1939

5   The old *Earl* from the Horse of Burravoe

6   Foredeck of old *Earl*

7   Burravoe flitboat alongside *St Clement* (II)

8 Second *Earl* in Burravoe

9 Second *Earl* at Hubie

10 Herring gutters, Lerwick, 1922

11 Herring station, Lerwick

12 Lerwick waterfront 1931

13 The Knab

which now stand empty and sometimes roofless, and by the complete depopulation not only of isolated spots like Westafirth (North Yell) or Setter (North Roe), but even of places adjoining main routes, like Dalsetter and Colvister (North Yell) and most of Houlland (South Yell). One result of improved transport has been the closing of many 'side schools', some of which consisted of no more than a one-roomed corrugated iron hut, of which the concrete foundations remain. I suppose that at one time wherever there were children more than three miles (the statutory walking distance) from the parish school a 'side school' had to be provided. Incidentally, when one recalls the remarkably high standards of literacy and hand-writing among many of the older generation of Shet-landers, one must marvel at the achievements of their teachers. While the tiny side schools have vanished, the local authority has made provision for other, more material, human needs by the erection at strategic points of public conveniences, something all but unknown in earlier years (though I recall a singularly primitive contraption projecting over the side of Linkshouse pier at Mid Yell). The bus shelters recently provided have come too late, when few people use public transport; they would have been far more useful a generation ago. Another way in which service has been given to travellers has been the provision of road-signs. Were there any road signs at all in Shetland when I first knew it? There were certainly none in Yell, and their systematic distribution all over Shetland, including the signposting of in-significant side roads, does not go very far back. (Official sign-posting seems to have taken a longer time to extend to islands elsewhere; on a visit to Bute in 1981 I noticed that the old-fashioned simple iron signs, without road-numbers, had not yet been superseded.) And Shetland did not, I think, possess any of those very old milestones one comes on quite frequently in Scotland, probably because when such milestones were erected Shetland as

yet had no roads. At a different level from public
conveniences, bus shelters and road-signs, has been the
proliferation of hotels. I suppose that in the 1920s and
1930s the only significant hotels outside Lerwick (which
had the Queen's and the Grand) were those at Spiggie,
Scalloway, Hillswick and latterly Sumburgh; now there
must be well over a dozen.

Lerwick as I first knew it was a small and compact
town, but clearly divided into four parts. There was the
old Lerwick of the sea-front, Commercial Street and the
picturesque lanes, huddled on the steep slope above
Bressay Sound. There was what might be called Victorian
Lerwick, spaciously laid out on the landward side of the
Hillhead, consisting mainly of impressive detached or
semi-detached villas — a fine piece of planning. Thirdly
was 'shanty-town', the straggle northwards of the herring
stations, each with its pier and its barracks for the gutters,
extending to Gremista, where the churches had their huts
in which, during the herring season, they ministered to
the gutters and tended the hands which suffered so much
from cuts and salt. Finally, council housing had just
started, at the north and south ends of Victorian Lerwick,
consisting of soundly and sensibly built little blocks which
fitted into the predominantly grey town. Nearly all the
landmarks of the 1920s do remain conspicuous —
Anderson Institute, Bruce Hostel, Widows' Homes, Post
Office, the numerous churches, the Town Hall — but
some of them have been swamped by new building and
collectively they are less significant in the vastly extended
town of today. Yet Lerwick, like Edinburgh, is to some
extent saved by its contours from the worst that modern
architects can do.

Beyond the south end of the town, where one can still
sit at the Knab beside the cemetery and the old gun-
emplacements and look away south towards Mousa and
across to Bressay Light, landscape and seascape have
hardly changed. It is actually a quieter scene, because you

do not see the fleet of steam drifters and sailing boats which you would have seen in the herring season in the 20s and 30s, and you will look in vain for the plume of smoke on the horizon which used to be the first sign of one of the mailboats coming up from Kirkwall or Aberdeen. It was from that vantage point that in 1939 I saw and photographed the new *Earl of Zetland* when she arrived, in convoy with three other North of Scotland ships: the last time I recall going out there to await the arrival of a ship was in 1959, when I was joining the *Tjaldur* to cross to Copenhagen and she was hours late coming from Faroe because of heavy weather. Now you are more likely to see planes and helicopters. If you look to the left, to the Ward of Bressay, you see the television masts on its shapely summit, and if you look back to the right you can see the tremendous growth of Lerwick beyond the Clickimin Loch and up the Scalloway road. And the cemetery, it need hardly be said, is very much fuller, with a lot of familiar names on the stones.

These reflections on changes and contrast may conclude with accounts of two recent experiences. One outstanding excursion came my way in 1980, when I was privileged to have a trip out from Sullom Voe on one of the pilot boats which serve incoming and outgoing tankers. I had hoped to do this in the previous year, but on the days when I was available and tankers were due the port was closed because of gales, and this taught me that I must seize an opportunity when it offered. It came in the form of a 'phone message to my hotel in Whiteness on Sunday morning about 8 o'clock, intimating that the pilot boat would be leaving at 9.15. Fortunately I was already out of bed, and dressing, so I got something in a bag to serve as breakfast and hared off north to Sellaness to join the pilot. I was no stranger to the waters of Yellsound, but my previous experiences had been of a very different kind. In 1931 I made the round, jogging along at eight knots, on the old *Earl,* from Burravoe, calling at Mossbank, Ollaberry, Bardister, Lochend, North Roe, Westsandwick and Ulsta. Twice I made a kind of circular tour of the sound in my own little boat at about six knots and I once made a return trip from Ulsta to North Roe in a chartered ferry boat at little more. To whiz out of Sullom Voe and up the sound at over 20 knots was exhilarating, and I felt it essential to keep my eyes ranging round all the time in order not to lose my orientation. We went north on the Mainland side, passing well to the west of Lamba and the other islands, right on until we were abreast of the Ramna Stacks, where we put a pilot aboard an incoming tanker. As we left her the obliging cox asked, 'Where do you want to go now?' and I modestly suggested we might return on a more easterly course, so we went down close to the west side of Muckleholm and Littleholm and then over to Little Roe, collecting a pilot from an outward-bound tanker on the way.

But while that experience showed dramatic change, another showed how much has remained blessedly unchanged. I began this chapter with my first expedition on arriving in Lerwick on a dull morning in 1977, and I can end it with what happened when I arrived on a different kind of morning in 1981. In May of that year, when it was a bright, sparkling day as I drove off the *St Clair*, my first objective was the extreme north-west of the Mainland. I left my car beside the graveyard on the shores of that splendidly sheltered haven, Sand Voe, and made out along the very wild coast which extends to the isle of Uyea. Out and back I walked for three and a half hours, with hardly a break except when I stopped for a quarter of an hour or so to watch four seals disporting themselves on and under the water of a deep gio and when I paddled in the water between the tidal isle of Uyea and the Mainland. And all the time I saw not a single sign of human activity on either land or sea except when I reached my destination and came on a shepherd working with his lambs. From that coast I was looking out over the track used by tankers approaching Yellsound and Sullom Voe, but there was nothing to be seen out there at all, where the ocean stretched unbroken to the Pole. The guiding lights which have been erected on the island of Grunay and the Point of Fethaland were the only signs that oil had come, the only changes since I had visited that remote area forty-five years before, in 1936.

2 Pleasures by Land: 'The Hill'

When my mother made her first visit to Shetland in 1922, she complained that 'You either walk one way along the road towards Ulsta or the other way along the road to Burravoe'. The weather had been wet, so that walking on the peat-moor of which Yell is largely composed would hardly have been possible, and we never took to 'the hill' — a phrase denoting all the land surface outside the enclosed townships. My nine-year-old legs would not have carried me on the extended hill-walks which became commonplace later, and I do not recall being much off the roads except for visits to the 'trout burn' and to the 'crö' where the sheep were being dipped. It is hardly surprising that my mother thought it a bit dull, for much of Shetland is dull if one keeps to the roads.

There was a great contrast when I paid my third visit in 1929, as an energetic senior schoolboy. I started that visit with nearly a fortnight in Lerwick, staying with cousins. They were, as they had been in my childhood, very good at taking me around, and I once walked across Bressay to Noss Sound with my cousin Jimmie (discoursing the while about Earl Patrick Stewart), but they were all at work and I was thrown largely on my own resources. I bought a Bartholomew's Half-Inch Map of 'Zetland' and began to explore. A map was necessary in those days even on the roads, in the absence of road signs, and it was with the roads that I started. I did the walk, so familiar to generations of Lerwegians, 'round the roads' — out the north road to the Brig o' Fitch and back by the

south road which came from Scalloway. (I amused my
cousins on my return by referring, too properly, to 'The
Bridge of Fitch'.) It was on that walk that I was for the
first time in a wheeled vehicle in Shetland, for a car
stopped and offered me a lift, which I gratefully accepted
and was carried down the hill to the road junction at the
Fitch burn, on a road which in those days was rather like
a pebbly beach. On another occasion I walked to Scalloway, to see for the first time the wonderful view from
The Scord and to inspect Earl Patrick's Castle, which
even then had some fascination for me, though at that
stage and for long after I knew little about the culture of
Jacobean Scotland which it represents. Forty years later,
in 1969, I held forth on the site to members of the
Historical Congress.

   More than once on that holiday I made use of the old
road over the Staney Hill behind Lerwick, which was
long familiar to me, and perhaps I began then to wonder
why no one has ever made a study of the old roads, so
clearly traceable in many parts of Shetland, which might
tell us much about the pattern of activity in earlier times.
I also revived — for I had been there as a small boy — the
pleasure of going out to the Knab, which for years was my
first stroll on every visit I paid to Lerwick and which more
recently has become a favourite spot at which to sit in my
car. But I branched out beyond modern roads, beyond
old roads and beyond defined paths. It was a novelty —
and my introduction to a pleasure which has been a
never-ceasing source of delight ever since (in many parts
of the world) — to explore a stretch of coast which was
completely new to me. This pleasure had a very modest
beginning: out to Rovi Head at the north end of Lerwick
harbour — then all untouched country beyond the fishing
stations at Gremista — and round to the Bight of
Vatsland and Kebister Ness. The coastline is unexciting
by Shetland standards, but it was my first acquaintance
with a coast in its purely natural state, as distinct from the

Knab, for instance, which had a path to it. It was on one of those walks north from Lerwick that I first experienced another pleasure for the first time — that of stripping and having an impromptu swim, taking advantage of my remoteness from any habitation.

Far better things were to come when, after that fortnight in Lerwick in 1929, I went on to Yell. There were walks out on the Ness of Lussetter, on the south side of Mid Yell voe (which I was later to know as the historic glebe of the vicars of Yell), but a far more enthralling prospect was opened up when I went on to Westsandwick and discovered the west side of Yell. I had heard it said that the best Shetland scenery is on the west side, and here it was. I still have a vivid recollection of the first time I came up to the summit at Scattlands, glimpsed the Ramna Stacks on the horizon and looked down on that wonderful panorama of the golden sandy wick, the breaking sea marking the skerry, the green-black of the broch, the holm, lying off, penetrated by a natural tunnel — a complex which I still think one of the most beautiful spots in the whole creation. I am glad I knew it so well before its glorious sand-dunes were devastated by greedy exploiters to meet the insatiable appetite of the concrete-mixers. And from Westsandwick I made far and away the most ambitious coastal exploration I had yet done — along the 'Neaps' or cliffs of Graveland to the Point of the Stuis, a stretch of rock-bound shore, rising to 400 feet, in its wildness rarely paralleled even in Shetland. One of the most conspicuous features of that coast is the Ern Stack, so called because it was formerly a nesting-place of the Ern or Sea Eagle. I have been told that the iron spikes driven into the rock by the miscreant who removed the last egg from the nest and thereby brought breeding to an end at this spot can still be seen, but despite close inspection (with binoculars) I am not convinced that I have ever succeeded in detecting them. There are indeed points on the rock-face from which trickles of red-rust colour descend, but this may arise from iron oxide in the rock. Besides, there have been substantial rock-falls over the years, and it is quite possible that the surface in which the spikes were originally inserted is now tumbled down with other debris at the foot of the stack.

The round of the 'Neaps' of Graveland is completed by walking south along the western shore of Whaalfjord, which, measuring five miles, is not the longest of Shetland voes but is surely one of the most shapely in its proportions. At this point I am torn between acclaiming the splendour of a particular coast and running the risk of encouraging too many others to explore it. On all the many occasions I have been round Graveland and Whaalfjord I do not think I have ever encountered another human being on the circuit. Perhaps it is as well that most writers, who are not enterprising enough to leave the main roads through Yell (many of which are dull) have endorsed Tudor's description of the island as 'wanting in scenic attractions' and have thereby discouraged tourists.

However, while those first visits to Mid Yell and Westsandwick have been followed, on all or almost all my later visits to Shetland, by so many more, my main base in Yell was at my ancestral home in Hamnavoe at the south end of the island. It was from Hamnavoe that for years I did most of my 'traivelling', to use the Shetland word for walking. Not only was there ample scope for 'traivelling', but there was little choice, even if one wanted to keep to the roads. Cars were scarce, and beyond the means of an impecunious schoolboy or student. The first car in the island — and he thought the second in Shetland — was brought in by Dr Taylor to Yell about 1903, but he found it so troublesome that he disposed of it and used a motor cycle instead until in 1912 he obtained a Model T Ford, which he followed by newer models throughout his long career. Perhaps because the Doctor had at one time had the island's roads (such as

C

they were) to himself, he was an excessively cautious or
timid driver, who preferred to stop on catching sight of
another car, unless the other driver paid him the
compliment of stopping instead. By 1929 there were car-
hirers in Mid Yell, Burravoe (where 'the car' was then a
novelty), Westsandwick and Cullivoe, but there were few
if any privately-owned cars except the Doctor's. Then
and for some years afterwards every car in the island was
known individually and some said they could identify
each of them by its characteristic sound, without seeing it.
One mail car, based in Westsandwick, did the round of
the southern half of the island, collecting mail from the
post-boxes, putting it aboard the steamer and conveying
the mail from the steamer to the local post-offices on the
return journey. Another mail car performed a similar
office in the northern half of the island. These cars carried
passengers as well as mail and provided useful con-
nections with the steamer on Monday and Friday and
with the ferry across Yellsound on Wednesday, when the
mail came by road from Lerwick to Mossbank and
crossed the sound to Ulsta. Until 1937, when the steamer
began to bring the mail on Tuesday evening, she did not
provide a connection with the direct boat arriving in
Lerwick on Tuesday, though on alternate Wednesdays
the *Earl* left Lerwick in the morning for her Yellsound
run, which included a call at Burravoe. It was therefore
only on a Wednesday that one was likely to be expecting a
friend to arrive with the mail car from Ulsta after
reaching Lerwick with the steamer from the south, and
we would watch for the first sight of the mail car as on
other days we waited for the first sight of the *Earl*. From
Lower Hamnavoe we could see her coming over the
summit of the road on her way from Ulsta; indeed we
glimpsed her briefly at the summit and then she disappeared from view in the dip at the Loch of Ulsta, to
reappear at the top of the long decline towards the
Arisdale Brig. The second sighting, even if the first

happened to be missed, allowed ample time, given her slow progress on a poor road, to meet her at the Kirk, where the track from Lower Hamnavoe reached the road and where she had to stop at the post-box in the kirkyard-dyke. Timing was especially important on a stormy day, for this was long before the era of bus-shelters.

Being myself a devotee of the steamer, I never went north from Lerwick on a Wednesday morning with the mail car, but on rare occasions, for journeys in Yell, I made use of the services — I might almost say the hospitality — of the mail car which served South Yell, and its genial driver Johnnie Leask. Motor bikes were more common than cars, and as one or two of my contemporaries owned them I had many a pillion ride from obliging friends. Sometimes I arranged with Robbie Hughson, who then ran the Hamnavoe shop, to meet me with his bike somewhere on the road back from Mid Yell in an evening, when I had walked there earlier in the day.

But in the main I got around on foot. Most people did in those days, and one of the most striking changes of the last few years is illustrated by the fact that when one drives around Shetland nowadays one hardly ever sees anyone walking and it is rare indeed — far rarer than it is in the south — to see anyone 'thumbing a lift'. Even in my young days, 'traivelling' was not quite as necessary as it had been in still earlier times. My great-uncle (born in 1844), once on receiving a telegram to join a ship and there being no suitable sailing of 'the little steamer', as he always called the *Earl,* shouldered his box and, after crossing Yellsound, walked the twenty-eight miles from Mossbank to Lerwick. In recent years my continued liking for 'traivelling' has sometimes been thought a shade eccentric, and anyone who walked now as I did in the thirties would probably be certified. Professor Tawney held that the first requirement for the study of economic history was a pair of stout walking boots. I might have learned as much as I ever did about Shet-

land's economic history without 'traivelling' as much as I
did, but I learned a lot of other things.

To 'traivel' to Mid Yell or Westsandwick was almost
a matter of routine, done times without number. Once, I
remember, I was commissioned to convey a message to
Dr Taylor in Mid Yell: no telephone in those days, and a
telegram from the post office at Burravoe, a couple of
miles from Hamnavoe, would not have met the case. I
almost always went over 'the hill' for at least part of those
journeys. Even between Hamnavoe and Burravoe I had
long learned that if one was heading for the shop and the
pier at Brough there was a short-cut 'through the Ness',
south of the Loch of Littlester, where there had been an
old road before the present road on the other side of the
loch was made. From Hamnavoe to Westsandwick it
would have been lunacy to follow the road all the way,
involving as it did a long detour right down to the shop at
Ulsta, and there was a very practicable route, partly
following the line of another old road, which left the
present road near the Loch of Ulsta and brought one over
the hill down into West Yell. It is a commentary on the
condition of the roads in those days that on two or three
occasions when I borrowed a bicycle for a trip from
Hamnavoe to Westsandwick I pushed the machine over
this rough short-cut instead of keeping to the road on its
detour by Ulsta. The bike's owner, it so happened, was a
Westsandwick man who had married a Hamnavoe
woman and the remark was made that the bike, after
much use by Geordie in his courting days, knew that
route well. Once, as little more than an experiment, I
avoided the road all the way between Hamnavoe and
Westsandwick, following the Arisdale Burn to its source,
traversing the Den of Noub and then descending the Burn
of Dalamut to the house called Moorbrae. This, however,
was a sheer waste of effort, as it involved so much walking
over rough ground. Besides, taking the short-cut by the
Loch of Ulsta over to West Yell and then following the

road carried the bonus of the wonderful view of Yellsound and its many islands which surely deserve, far more than the barren rocks of the Firth of Forth, Sir Walter's phrase, 'like emeralds chased in gold'. There were then on those waters no oil tankers with their attendant pilot boats and tugs.

There was a larger number of practicable routes between Hamnavoe and Mid Yell. As in walking to Westsandwick, I think I only once kept to the hill all the way, up the Burn of Hamnavoe and down the Burn of Laxa. It made better sense to use the road for part of the journey. At the Hamnavoe end I took to the hill from the start, except on one occasion at Eastertide, when, as the hill was very wet after snow, I followed the road all the way except for cutting a corner at Kettlester, Burravoe. It was possible to use the hill for a relatively short distance, crossing by the north end of the Loch of Kettlester, but one could hold to the hill by a variety of more northerly routes and come down to the road at different points from Gossabrough to Otterswick. My favourite track was one that I used on my frequent visits to friends in Gossabrough, namely along the smooth east side of the hill called Blaafiel, then over some rather broken ground on the watershed and finally down a burn which led directly to the Gossabrough side-road. The stretch of road going to Mid Yell was on the whole dreary, but — taking the upper road, which was then regarded as the main route but now has subsidiary status — it was rather exciting to reach the point where I looked down into Mid Yell Voe, lying so snug among the hills. I rarely if ever walked to Mid Yell by the low road, which skirts Aywick and traverses a dull patch of low-lying land, but in recent years I have nearly always (like everyone else) driven over it and have come to appreciate the spectacle it affords above Vatster: looking over Hascosay, the north of Fetlar, a scatter of holms, the southern shores of Unst and away north to the twin heights of Vallafield and

Saxavord, it is one of the finest panoramas of the typical
Shetland intermingling of land and water. On the way
south from Mid Yell there was a pleasure to the eye of
which I never weary — a great double bay, comprising
Otterswick and the sandy, sheltered nook of
Gossabrough, bisected by that shapely peninsula,
Swarister. To the south lay the range of the East Yell cliffs
— the Ness of Gossabrough (50 feet), the White Hill (100
feet), the Horse of Burravoe (200 feet) and the heights of
Ramnagio (300 feet), rising rhythmically, like a
symphony in four movements — and there was the view
out to the west banks of Fetlar and away to Skerries on the
horizon.

The walks to Westsandwick and Mid Yell were walks
with an objective, always to visit friends, sometimes to
spend a day or two with them. But there were many other
expeditions through the hills of South Yell, exploring the
long Hamnavoe and Arisdale burns and their tributaries,
in country which prompted an earlier writer to think of
Yell as 'a vast Serbonian bog'. It constitutes one of the
widest expanses of moorland in Shetland, and one is
almost surprised that such a featureless landscape should
have so many place-names, weird as they look:
Stouraclev, Lunga Skolla, Sundrabister (which was
surely once a settlement in the heart of the hills), Birries
Houlla Komba and Willa-mina Hoga. The last at least is
capable of interpretation: it is 'Woll-mennis-hoga', the
area where the scattalds or grazings of several townships
met to form a kind of no man's land, or rather every
man's land, derived from *almenning,* meaning common
land, and *hagi,* an enclosure. Often, too, I made for the
summits which provided good viewpoints — the nearby
Blaafiel and the Hamars of Houlland and the more
distant Ward of Arisdale and Hill of West Yell, from each
of which much of Shetland was displayed.

Normally it was all solitude as far as human beings
were concerned. Some of my routes, especially the one to

West Yell by the Loch of Ulsta and the old road, and the one to Mid Yell by the Loch of Kettlester, were recognised standard tracks which had been regularly used. The second, indeed, was a regular route for a special reason: the bull resided in East Yell and when the Hamnavoe kye required his services they were led over that familiar stretch of hill. Yet, even so, I do not recall ever meeting anyone in the course of my 'traivelling' over the hills. In the later part of the Second World War and subsequently there was what must have been unprecedented 'traivelling' on the hill west of the Arisdale Burn, to view 'the plane' — the remains of a bomber which had crashed there in 1942 with the loss of most of its Canadian crew. Surely never before had so many human feet trodden that particular waste — and never before had so many artefacts been carried away from the hill to various homes.

The Yell hills do not provide the easiest walking, for the stretches of firm, heather-covered turf have, interspersed among them, many patches of boggy 'green mires' which would take one up to the knees and some of which are really dangerous, as well as areas where centuries of erosion have cut deep gulleys in the peat. While the mires must be either circumvented or jumped over, the gulleys must usually be jumped, especially as they, too, often have soft and damp stretches at their bottoms, though when they are too wide to jump there is no alternative but to clamber down into them. A walk on the Yell hills was always something of a hop, skip and jump. I recall a remark of the late Brucie Henderson, who had every right to comment on the Yell hills, because from his home at Arisdale in the heart of them he was accustomed to make a bee line for any house he wanted to visit, regardless of the roads. As we strode along together — I trying to keep pace with his exceptionally long strides and he, I suspect, deliberately lengthening his each time I succeeded — he remarked, 'the hills are greatly deteriorated since I was a boy'. ('Deteriorated' was one of his favourite words.) I replied, rather thoughtlessly and casually, 'Oh, do you think so, Brucie?', to which he firmly put me in my place, 'I don't think, I know'. He may have been right, but very likely the deterioration was not in the hills but in Brucie's legs, which no longer carried him over the gulleys as they once had done. Brucie and anyone else with a similarly intimate knowledge of the hills would follow a precise track on which every possible obstacle was noted and duly marked in the mind. This was said to be particularly true, according to a story I was told in Fetlar, of Laurence Williamson, in whom familiarity with the hills was as conspicuous as his remarkable scholarship. A youth and a girl, in the hill one night as it had become dark, heard footsteps approaching and jumped down into a deep gulley. As the footsteps came nearer, they heard a voice, 'One, two, three, four and then a jump', and Laurence went sailing through the air above their heads. He had marked his position from some conspicuous white stone and measured his paces from it. (To introduce an irrelevance, I must here relate another story told me by the same informant. There was, so I was told, a man in Fetlar called Tammy Arnot, who had been at the Greenland whaling, where he had lost a toe through frostbite. Years later, someone recalling him asked, 'Tell me, did Tammy Arnot spell his name wi' ae tae or wi' twa?' and received the answer, 'Na, Tammy spelled his name wi' ae tae, Ah, err, enn, oh, tae,' and then, with hardly a pause and with unconscious humour, 'Ye ken, Tammy Arnot lost ane o' his taes at Greenland'.)

Despite the story of the Shetlander who, asked how he had found his way around London on his first visit, replied, 'I just used a chart and a compass', it appeared to be something of a mystery to the folk how I managed to make my way through those trackless wastes of Yell. To allay anxiety that I might get lost, I made it a habit never to disclose in advance where I was making for, and rather relished the exclamations when I returned and announced where I had been. Of course my immediate neighbours and close acquaintances, who thought of me as 'just one of us' (as one of them was to say, years later, when he congratulated me on my appointment to a professorial chair), soon ceased to marvel, and their attitude came to be expressed not as 'Where have you been?' but 'Is there anywhere you have not been?' But casual visitors to South Yell from other parts of Shetland, who thought me a 'sooth man', took a different view. When one of my host's brothers arrived one day and expressed a wish to go on 'the hill', he was told, 'Oh, Gordon will take you', and replied, 'I don't want to get lost'. Later on, when that same visitor expressed a wish to go off in a boat and again was told, 'Oh, Gordon will take you', he replied. 'I don't want to go on a rock'. My host (who once flattered me by saying, 'I'd go to Lerwick in a boat wi' Gordon wi' lockit e'en') laughed him to scorn. But no later criticism of my historical scholarship has ever wounded me so deeply as the remarks of that visitor did nearly fifty years ago.

A lot of my 'traivelling' was not inland, not strictly on 'the hill', but rather along 'the banks' — a term used to mean almost any type of shore, but especially, as 'high banks', the cliffs. And I walked again and again around the rocky, often precipitous, shores of Yell. The pleasure of walking along any shore for the first time is great, but 'the banks' of Shetland's coastline have their peculiar fascination. The variety is endless, for every few yards reveal some new curiosity in the shape of a cave, a gio, a natural arch or a tunnel, fantastically shaped stacks or offshore peaked rocks. There is an element of frustration in one's inability to see as much from the shore as one could from a boat, but the constant change beckons one on, and one walks and scrambles on tirelessly. The exploration of 'the banks' by sea is another matter, for another chapter.

For many years — most of the pre-war years — the
bulk of my 'traivelling' was done in Yell, because I
seldom spent much time in any other part of Shetland.
However, besides exploring every mile — almost every
yard — of the coast of Yell, I was able to cover Fetlar
thoroughly, for I spent a few days there on more than one
occasion. Fetlar, I soon discovered, is a splendid island
for walking, because a lot of the surface consists of firm,
dry ground, singularly free from irregularities. Apart
from a strip on the west, which has close affinities with
Yell on the other side of Colgrave Sound, it could hardly
present a greater contrast to that nearby island. Mr
Carson, the Fetlar minister, used to say, 'I can never
understand why anyone lives in Yell when you can get to
Fetlar for a couple of bob' (two shillings being the single
steerage fare on the old *Earl* from Mid Yell to Brough
Lodge). The most serious obstacles to the walker on
Fetlar are man-made, in the shape of high and soundly-
constructed dykes and well-maintained post-and-wire
fences. The ramparts of cliff on the north and west, which
look so impressive viewed from Unst and Yell respectively, are somewhat disappointing at close quarters, for
they are far from being perpendicular and do not have
many features of interest in detail, but elsewhere in the
island there is a great deal of variety well worthy of close
examination. The east coast from the Snap to the Brough
of Strand is impressive in its bare wildness, and the coast
around the Clett, that miniature of the Bass Rock, is as
rugged as you will find anywhere. Perhaps the bit of the
Fetlar coast that has most natural curiosities in a short
stretch is the west side of the Wick of Gruting, south from
the Clett: there are fine arches opposite the Clett and at
the Ruvrapund, and the Kirn o' Gjula is in effect a cave
with a large vent opening through the roof to the sky.

Besides visits to Fetlar, I had a splendid weekend in
Unst in 1932. I arrived at Baltasound on the Friday
evening in a thick fog, when the old *Earl* almost ran on the

head of Huney on her passage from Uyeasound, and on Saturday morning, when the fog showed signs of lifting, we set out for Burrafirth. One of the unforgettable sights of my life was that of the sun breaking through the banks of fog which still hung heavily around the massive cliffs on both sides of the Firth and magnified their grandeur. We proceeded on the classic walk across Hermaness to the point where we could look down on the Flugga. It was there that I first encountered the bonxies or Great Skuas, which were rarer then than they have become since, when they are familiar enough on many of the moorlands in Shetland. In recent years I have been aware of them particularly between Lumbister and Colvister in Yell and in the northern part of Fetlar. Once almost extinct, these birds have multiplied exceedingly under protection, and some would say that it is the humans who now have more need of protection against the alarming aggressive tactics of those splendid creatures. A walking stick, preferably of a light type which is not tiring to hold above one's head, is a useful defence, and people have been known to strap a cane across their shoulders, so that it projects well above the head, with the same purpose as a barrage baloon.

On the Sunday of that weekend in Unst we were at Haraldswick, Norwick and Skaw and climbed Crucifiel. An unexpected and memorable pleasure was a visit to Mrs Jessie M. E. Saxby, then aged ninety but still writing books. It was possibly the first time that the nineteen-year-old student had had tea with a real live author — and one so remarkable in many ways. A daughter of Dr Edmondston, she had been widowed at an early age by the death of her husband, Dr Saxby, and had brought up her family by her pen. She wrote a number of novels which she candidly regarded as pot-boilers and which were set in various parts of the country. One of them, *Preston Tower*, was, by a curious coincidence, given to me by my maternal grandmother some time in the 1920s and remained in my possession — as it still does — when for four-and-a-half-years I lived in a house in the shadow of Preston Tower. But Mrs Saxby also devoted herself to pieces about Shetland history and folklore. *The Home of a Naturalist*, containing essays by her and her brother, Biot Edmondston, is a book of singular charm in its unaffected way, and her late work, *Shetland Traditional Lore* (1932), is of lasting value. She was, all else apart, a real link with the past. When I was discoursing to my students on the reliability of memory and the transmission of information by word of mouth, I used to tell them that I once met an old lady whose father was born in 1795. Of course there was nothing exceptional in that for anyone of my generation, but it startled the students. After that 1932 visit I was hardly in Unst again, except for brief visits to Muness and Uyeasound in the course of my boating expeditions (described in chapter 4), until after the War.

The only other significant islands I saw much of before the War were Bressay (on several visits) and Noss. To walk over Noss and climb to the top of the Noup, as I did in 1932, made me crave to see that 600-foot cliff from the sea. Twice I was frustrated when I hoped to circumnavigate it on the local steamer, for on the first occasion the excursion was cancelled because of fog and on the second because of heavy weather. I later fulfilled my ambition to view Noss from the sea, but on larger craft — the *Regina Maris* and the *Uganda* — but not until May 1983 did I complete the circumnavigation, when the *St Clair* made a special cruise. Apart from the early expeditions on foot from Lerwick I did little walking on the Mainland in the 1930s except as an activity subsidiary to the boating expeditions described in chapter 4. After the war my Mainland 'traivelling' was again mainly subsidiary, but now to the trips I was making by car — either a hired one or my own.

There was no point in taking my own car to Shetland until after the vehicle ferry to Yell arrived in 1973, and I first did so in 1975. Before that I sometimes had self-driven hired cars. The first time I hired one was in 1962, when I took my parents north on what I knew would be their last visit to Shetland. We had a car in Lerwick from Tuesday to Saturday and made good use of it — Sumburgh, Mousa, Eshaness (for the first time), North Roe and Toft (so that we could cross on the passenger ferry and have a day in Yell). Thereafter I hired a car in Yell on three or four occasions when I was going to be there for a few days, and each time found illustrations of the delightfully informal way in which business was still transacted. The car would be waiting for me on the pier at Mid Yell when I landed from the steamer, and I simply left it at Ulsta when I crossed the sound from Yell on my way south: no questions asked, no forms filled in, and the cheque for the hire laid on the driving seat of the car when I left it at Ulsta.

In earlier days I had very occasionally hired a car with a driver. I first did this, with my mother and sister, in 1930, when we were in Lerwick and we had a drive to visit friends at Waas and at the Sandsting Manse. In South Yell 'the car' usually meant one thing and one thing only, the car driven by Bobby Hugh (R. H. Williamson), who took me back and forward between Burravoe and Hamnavoe times without number between 1930 and 1950, when I was arriving or departing by the steamer, at a cost pre-war of 3/-. The great expedition was to hire Bobby Hugh for a day and have an outing the whole length of Yell, to Gloup and back — 25/-.

As long as Burravoe was one of the steamer's ports of call I was normally joining or leaving her there and did not need to use the mail car (which connected with her at Mid Yell). But when I went north at Christmas 1933 and her schedule, as usually then on a Thursday in winter, was from Skerries to Mid Yell — a beautifully calm trip on Christmas Eve — I intended to go on to Burravoe by the mail car, but it happened that Bobby Hugh had brought a hire to Mid Yell and came on board the steamer, in the hope of getting another hire back. He asked if I wanted him, and I explained that for economy's sake I preferred to wait for the mail car, but when he failed to find another hire he said he would take my cousin Barbara Hughson and me to Burravoe and Hamnavoe for the mail-car fare. When I arrived at 'the Kirk', on a mild evening, Johnnie said 'It would have been more like the thing if you had stepped out and been up to your backside in snow'. But, as I was to discover, Shetland is apt to get its snow much later, and not least in April. And on Christmas day in Shetland that year I was out with neither hat nor coat.

After the War I made the circuit of Whalsay on foot one day, taking advantage of an excursion by the *Earl* which was designed to give people in the North Isles a chance to spend a few hours in Lerwick, but after joining the steamer at Burravoe I left at Symbister and rejoined her on her way north in the evening. The island hardly has the most exciting of shores, even on the east side, but offers wonderful views. Perhaps Whalsay is an island to look out from rather than to look at. Nearly all the parts of Unst which I had not seen previously I covered when it became my practice to make the most of the *Earl* in her later days and frequently spent a night on board in Baltasound. It was on the first of those occasions that I reached the top of Saxavord and got a new and striking view of the Flugga lying below, as well as to the south and south-west over Unst, Yell and Northmavine — all seen in the waning light of an April day when there had been many snow showers around, and looking like the fading splendour of an old oil painting. On other similar visits to Unst the Rev Douglas Lamb took me to Burrafirth on a golden evening and to the Westing and the Old Kirk at Lund.

The most important completely novel piece of coastal walking I did after the War was in Papa Stour. That was an island which had fascinated me at a distance,

as it were, every since I had learned, in my very earliest
forays into elementary Shetland history, that the name
meant 'The great island of the priests' (and not, as a joker
suggested, 'Dust of our fathers'). Later on, but still long
before I visited that delectable island, I had put it in its
context as one of the early religious settlements on the
western fringes of the British Isles and had come to realise
that, just as Inchcolm has been called 'The Iona of the
East', so Papa Stour might claim to be 'The Iona of the
North'. When the Norsemen came to Shetland, they are
supposed to have given the name 'Papa' or 'Priests' Isle'
to three islands on which they found Christian monks
established, and the largest was distinguished as 'Stour'
or 'Great'. No traces remain of that early religious
settlement, and few antiquities at all, beyond indeterminate cairns and mounds, were recorded by the
Royal Commission in its *Inventory* (for which the
surveying was done about 1930). The 'Hellifiel' or Holy
Hill is as likely to take its name from pagan as from
Christian associations. On the south side are the
foundations of a somewhat shapeless enclosure and
remains which it is tempting to identify with burial sites
but which are as likely to be the 'steeds' or foundations for
piles of dried turf. Forewick Holm, off the north-east
coast of Papa, has the remains of what was plainly a
defensive structure, a semi-circular wall across a
promontory and clearly defined foundations within it.
Recent excavations on Papa, initiated by Dr Barbara
Crawford, have given some confirmation to its claim to
have been an important secular centre in medieval times,
in the days of the Norse earldom of Orkney, but its earlier
history remains obscure.

Yet speculation as to the historic significance of this
Great Island of the Priests is encouraged by its
remarkable resemblance to Iona. The two islands are
almost identical in area (3-3 ½ square miles), each rises to
a height of about 300 feet; in each case, low, green shores,

bordering a sound less or more than half a mile wide, are washed by the clear waters of the Atlantic, which take on a green hue from the sand. The great promontory of the Shetland Mainland which terminates at Sandness is not unlike the Ross of Mull, and to the north the great sweep of St Magnus Bay is so similar in proportions to the broad inlet on the west side of Mull — each about 10 miles across — that when the outlines are compared they almost coincide. One need only lay down a map of Shetland alongside a map of Argyll to see how striking the similarity is. Everything combines to recall St Columba's Isle and to prompt the query whether Papa was in early times indeed a northern Iona but escaped those later developments which created the notable buildings on the island in the west.

I at last managed to spend a few days in Papa in 1952, when I systematically 'quartered' the island, starting on each expedition from the house where I was staying and covering, section by section, the wonderful coast. I already knew that Papa, although lying so close to the Mainland, shared the problems which had caused the evacuation of more remote islands. The sound which separates it from Sandness, at the end of the thirty-mile road from Lerwick, is less than a mile wide, but is liable to be swept by heavy Atlantic seas and powerful tide races. To make matters worse, landing facilities were still poor. At Sandness there was only the open beach, exposed to the north and north-west; the shore of Papa directly opposite has likewise only open beaches, while exposed promontories hinder access to the sheltered Housa Voe, which had a pier, though one that was of little use except at high water — 'built on dry land' it was unkindly said. Most shipping of goods, passengers and mails had therefore to be by open boats; even when a decked vessel was used, it was too often necessary to tranship everything to a small boat for conveyance to and from the shore.

On the day I left the island it happened that a wedding party was arriving. The bride and bridegroom had been married in Lerwick in the morning, and drove to Sandness in the afternoon with many of their guests, for there was to be a reception in the island schoolroom. I had left the beach opposite Sandness in an open boat, and a motor fishing-boat, coming round from Housa Voe, met it to tow it across the sound — a pleasant way of travelling, for it is all too rare to achieve a reasonable speed with a complete absence of vibration. At Sandness, while the fishing-boat anchored, the small boat went to the beach to serve as a 'tender'. But even so, all the members of the wedding party, including the bride, had to be unceremoniously carried pick-a-back off the sands. Two boat loads were ferried out to the motor-boat, which then took the small boat in tow with a third load. Fortunately there was a light offshore breeze, or the operation would have been singularly uncomfortable, and fatal to wedding garments.

Deposits of peat, never very deep, did exist in Papa, as old workings show, but all of it was used up in the days when the island supported a population which rose in 1841 to 382. Its removal was followed by erosion, which over a large part of the island laid bare the rock, and elsewhere, except in the cultivated areas, left only scanty soil. Some of the turf, thin and sandy as it was, had been cut and used for burning, but the main fuel was coal, which was costly even then (though it was cheaper in Papa than in the North Isles). As is general throughout Shetland, while cattle-rearing had declined, sheep stocks had increased; the resulting imbalance between the two was unhealthy, for, as a local spokesman put it, 'Sheep destroy the grazing'. Cultivation had greatly receded, and Papa, like so many islands, told the dismal story of the abandonment of many 'rigs' which generations of men and women had toiled to make, and to keep, productive. It was poor compensation, even to an

D

antiquary, that Papa was one of the few places where some Shetland mills, with their horizontal water-wheels, were still in working order.

The population had continued to decline: at the time of my visit it was little more than sixty, and the family which gave me accommodation was on the point of leaving for New Zealand. There was a certain seasonal or temporary loss when young men went off to National Service, the Merchant Navy or (as they were doing in the early 1950s) the Antarctic whaling, and already the manning of the mailboat threatened to become a critical problem. The situation was not helped by educational requirements which, in so many places, involved the removal of children, at the age of twelve, for schooling on the Mainland. Uprooted from their rural, insular surroundings and taken to a town for an urban education, they never returned to settle in the island; and some parents, rather than have the family unit disrupted, leave for the Mainland when their children go. The comment heard in Papa in 1952, as it was heard so generally then throughout the islands, was 'This place is dying', and when a community is robbed of its young people its death cannot be long deferred.

The cliffs of Papa never greatly exceed 200 feet in height, and judged by that alone would be inconspicuous in a land of precipices like Shetland, but the shores have two uncommon merits. The rocks are red — pink felsite and red sandstone — and this colour is enriched by vivid green grass on the cliff tops and yellow and grey lichen on their sides. The other notable feature is that the cliffs are perpendicular, sometimes columnar, presenting sharp vertical faces to the sea, and the stacks, or rocks isolated from the parent cliffs, are often as clear-cut as if they had been artificially hewn. They closely resemble the rocks of Handa, off the Sutherland coast.

Although the island measures less than three miles across, there are so many indentations, in voes and gios, that the length of the coast is estimated at from 22 to 25 miles, and the visitor who spends a few days working over it in sectors finds it of unending interest. The caves for which the island is famous can be entered only by boat, as is usually so in Shetland, where the land is everywhere sinking. Those easiest of access are in the north-east corner of the island, and I was fortunate enough to be able to borrow a boat and explore them (and also to land on Forewick Holm). Going through an archway which must represent an earlier cave but is now isolated through the fall of a roof, and entering the present cave, a 'junction' is reached from which different passages can be explored. Looking back from this point the view is arresting, for beyond the mouth of the cave is the isolated arch, and it in turn frames an outlying stack. From the 'junction' a short passage to the right leads out to the open, while to the left is a longer and more tortuous tunnel which again leads ultimately to daylight.

For visits to the caves weather conditions require to be such as seldom occur on that exposed coast, for there are submerged rocks and tidal streams, there is the danger of falling rock, and any form of artificial light serves only to 'make darkness visible'. Not many of the men I met on the island had any recent experience of the caves, and the intimate knowledge of them which used to be current may be lost, but the enterprising Tudor left a full description of them. The Great Hole of Bordie runs for about half a mile through a peninsula, and one of the islets is said to have a main tunnel running through from north to south and two others traversing the first at right angles. Kirstan Hole, on the south coast, can be appreciated without a boat. A gio over a hundred yards long and with sides about 100 feet high leads from the open sea to a tunnel of some forty yards; beyond this the cave roof has collapsed, leaving an open gully another hundred yards in length; beyond this again there is a continuation of the cave for, it is said, 70 or 80 yards.

The great arch at the Horn of Papa, one of the finest in Shetland, was swept away by a gale in the winter after I saw it, but many others remain.

On most of the cliffs the sea-birds have a tenancy which is seldom disturbed. The now ubiquitous fulmars are the most conspicuous, their fluffy chicks (in late July) on ledges and often quite accessible, while the parents, deserting their young at the approach of a stranger, constantly glide to and fro. At a point west of Culla Voe I had a close view of a party of black guillemots, on the flank of a stack rising from the middle of a gio. Their sooty plumage, extending to their heads, contrasted sharply with the white patch on the wings and with the red feet, which seemed disproportionately large. From time to time a mouth opened revealing a brilliant red interior and emitting a sound something between a squawk and a whistle, represented by the bird's Shetland name, 'tystie'. The greater black-backs had taken possession of the table-like Liri Skerry (which takes its name from the Shetland name for the Manx shearwater). I saw only one pair of great skuas, and a few Arctic skuas. There were many oystercatchers, the terns were numerous, noisy and irritable. A few gannets could be seen off the west side, and the usual shags were perched on peaked rocks.

Papa Stour affords fine views of the rugged west side of Shetland. To the north, St Magnus Bay sweeps round from Eshaness lighthouse by those stately rocks the Dore Holm and the Drongs to Urafirth and Hillswick, with Roeness Hill above them; and on to its eastern shores, the rocks diversified by the red cliffs which gave its name to Muckle Roe (the Big Red Island). Away to the south-west is Foula, some seventeen miles distant, with its 1200 feet high cliffs, a mighty bastion against the western ocean. To the north-west, three or four miles off, but seemingly much closer from Papa's highest cliffs near the Horn, lie the Vee Skerries, which will always recall the wreck of the trawler *Ben Doran* to those whose memories go back to April 1930. At that time the nearest lifeboat was at Stromness, and by the time it arrived the seas had so risen that although seven men could be seen clinging to the rigging nothing could be done except to stand by and watch them drop off one by one. It was said that no life was ever saved from a ship wrecked on the Vee Skerries — but that was before the advent of the helicopter. In calm weather they stand out conspicuously enough from the sea — indeed it is not difficult to land, and in Papa I was shown photographs which had been taken on the skerries — but when the Atlantic swell comes in they disappear in a smother of spray and foam.

It may safely be claimed for Papa that nowhere else can more fine and varied cliff scenery be found within a comparable area. Taking its beautiful situation, its wonderful coast and its historic associations, there is no doubt that if it were more accessible it would be over-run by trippers. As attractive in many ways as that other, better-known, Iona, it would have been as great a mecca for tourists had it been put 'on the map' in the way that the daily steamer from Oban used to make the western Iona an indispensable objective for all visitors.

Next in importance to Papa Stour among my post-war discoveries I would put Muckle Roe. I had seen its unexciting eastern shores from the water when I traversed Roe Sound by boat, and on a later occasion I had driven across the bridge and admired the view looking out the sound to the north-west, but it was not until 1978 that I walked right over to the west side, where the red cliffs are unquestionably one of the most attractive corners of the Shetland coast. How odd that Papa Stour has retained the Norse adjective meaning 'big', whereas Muckle Roe has had its adjective Scotticised. But on the seventeenth-century map it is still 'Ru Oy Stour', and the 'Ru Oy' represents not a bad attempt to indicate the subtleties of the native pronunciation.

In the same year as I visited the west side of Muckle
Roe I was on yet another of Shetland's western isles,
Vaila. For this visit I was indebted to the courtesy of the
proprietor in not only taking me across the sound but in
showing me over his very remarkable residence, where an
old Shetland laird's house was transformed at the end of
last century into a splendid Victorian castellated
mansion. The place it most reminded me of was Kinloch
Castle, in Rum. I wondered if a tower nearer the cliffs
might represent the 'fortalice' which an earlier laird was
permitted to erect in the 1570s to protect the island from
raiders from the Western Isles, but none of the visible
work could be of such antiquity. I think Vaila completed
my tally of the inhabited islands of Shetland, leaving aside
the lighthouse islands of Bound Skerry and Muckle
Flugga. Uninhabited islands are a matter for another
chapter, on my boating excursions.

The frustration I sometimes felt when I was exploring a stretch of cliffs on foot and wished I had had a
boat handy to investigate them more closely may have
been a factor in stimulating me into acquiring a boat. But
after I got a boat there were still areas where I walked
along 'the banks' either because I did not have my own
boat at hand or was not able to borrow one. Thus the
exploration of Shetland's rocky shores by land is
something that has continued throughout my life.
Anyone who wants to appreciate Shetland to the full must
realise that the key to access to many of its most attractive
stretches is simply the ability to use one's legs. There is
seldom good cliff scenery in immediate proximity to
roads, and much of the best cliff scenery is far from any
road. This applies, for instance, to Graveland, the north
of Unst, Papa Stour, Muckle Roe and even Eshaness. I
twice walked round Eshaness, which is perhaps the most
publicised part of the Shetland coast. It is fine, but not as
outstanding by Shetland standards as is apt to be
believed, and it might never have achieved its reputation

if nearby Hillswick had not for so long been a leading tourist centre.

After all the intermittent effort of sixty years — including of course many repeated visits to favourite areas — there are still worlds left to conquer. I have never been on the top of Fitful Head, for example, I have not seen as much as I ought of the coast of Waas and Sandness, and I have not been over at the cliffs on the west side of Roeness Hill. It was only in 1982 that I fully appreciated some of the delights of the rocky shores in the area to the west of the road just north of the Mavis Grind, where sheltered voes like Mangaster and Gunnister open out almost directly into the wide open sea of St Magnus Bay. The attractions there rival those of the area around Clousta and West Burrafirth.

Exploring 'the banks' has some affinities to historical research, to the extent that with experience one gains new insights and even becomes aware of problems which demand investigation. Thus in the last couple of years I have invented a new hobby — 'collecting Birriers'. I had been aware from my early days of the Birrier a mile or so north of Westsandwick. It consists of a mass of rock with a fairly flat top (well clad in grass) sloping to seaward and joined to the parent cliff by a neck or isthmus which might be called a saddle. This, broad enough at sea-level, narrows upwards, with steep, grass-covered flanks, to little more than a razor-edge, on which a curious peak of rock obtrudes. I have met Westsandwick men who had made their way across, but this achievement would require exceptional nerve and would seem to be best left to a cragsman with some equipment. It has always been known that the Birrier itself has some remains on it, presumably prehistoric or dark age, and of course access from the land may well have been easier in earlier times. Almost as long as I have been familiar with this formation I have been aware also of another Birrier, on the other side of Yell, about a mile south of Vatster. Here again

there is a grass-covered table-like promontory beyond a
narrow isthmus, but this time the isthmus is penetrated
by a natural arch. As at Westsandwick the neck is very
narrow at the top, but it is almost level with the adjacent
cliffs and is much shorter, so that a couple of steps on the
razor-edge take one across. Even so, I once felt I could
not risk even those two steps when a strong cross-wind
was blowing, and returned next day in quieter conditions.
There are a number of stones among the vegetation on
this Birrier, and it, too, might have had some early
structure on it. On the entrance to both of those Yell
Birriers fencing is erected in the hope of keeping sheep off
grazing which they must find tempting but which might
lead them into danger and put them beyond their owners'
reach.

I pondered the possible association between those
Birriers and the signs of early occupation of sites like the
Clett and the Outer Brough of Strand in Fetlar. The Clett
is a completely detached rock and so now is the Brough,
but at one point the channel between the Outer Brough
and the Inner Brough is both narrow and shallow,
suggesting the likelihood that in the not too distant past
there was a formation like those Birriers. There is,
incidentally, no water on the Outer Brough of Strand — a
point to be kept in mind in connection with the whole
question of human occupation. However, in assessing the
Clett and the Brough of Strand I discovered that Fetlar
also has two Birriers, one south of Funzie and the other
west of the Clett.

The former, on the south side of Muckle Birrier Gio,
conforms to the Yell specimens to the extent of having a
large 'table-top' of grass, but the isthmus here is a very
wide one, so that there is no problem of access and of
course no need to try to exclude sheep. There are no
visible remains of foundations on the Birrier, but one or
two earth-bound stones on the isthmus suggest that there
might have been some defensive work there at one time.
At the Birrier beside the Clett, the access — or lack of

14   The North Mouth, Lerwick, about 1930

15   The North Mouth 1983

16 Vaila House

17 Sand

18 The 'Roost', Lerwick

19 Bank Lane, Lerwick

20 Scalloway Castle 1983

21 The Horn, Papa Stour

22 Papa Stour

23 Burravoe about 1930

24 Burravoe 1981

25 Mavis Grind about 1930

26 Mavis Grind 1982

27 Papa Stour

28 Graveland Banks

access — conforms to that of the Westsandwick Birrier. Here the Birrier rock itself is very rugged and lacks the flat top and the vegetation which the three others have. It is inconceivable that there can ever have been any kind of habitation on it, unless the configuration of the land has altered greatly. Altogether, therefore, I conclude that the term Birrier, whatever its etymology, is given to those four different rocks because of the physical formation and not because of any use by man. I had not formulated this idea when I last saw a fifth Birrier, which gives it name to Burrier Wick at the approach of Uyea (Northmavine), but my impression is that it resembles the Birrier beside the Clett. Speculations like this add spice to the endless fascination of visiting and revisiting the shores of the islands. But even if such speculation does not intrude, a man who walks along almost any part of the Shetland coast, especially for the first time, will assuredly be rewarded.

Until after the Second World War most of the roads were simply deplorable by southern standards. Tarring apparently started on the road between Lerwick and Sumburgh and I have been told that it had reached Cunningsburgh by 1939. The old waterbound roads turned to mud and potholes in wet weather and to something like beaches in a drought. Not only so, but the engineering was primitive, for they switch-backed up and down from one burn to the next. I suppose they were made that way to save labour in creating banking or cuttings and to save expense in building anything more than the absolute minimum of a bridge — either a wooden structure or a culvert above which turves were laid to bring up the road level. This was all especially true in the North Isles, where anything in the way of road-making machinery was slow in coming, partly because of the difficulty of transporting it by the steamer and landing it on islands without piers where the steamer could come alongside. There was always a danger that those old

bridges would be carried away when there was flood-
water, and this happened from time to time in Yell in the
twenties and thirties. Where a road has been realigned in
recent times it has usually been made to cross the burn at
a lower point, with a higher bridge, less of a decline and
incline and less of a bend at the bridge. When the tarred
roads came they were much less satisfactory for
pedestrians on a dark night, for the lighter surface of the
waterbound roads showed up better.

The old roads, as I hinted earlier, were peculiarly
unsuited to cycling. I was not a very practised cyclist at
any period in my life, and two experiences in Shetland
remain in my mind. In 1932 on the way north I fell in
with a German medical student and we fixed up in the
same boarding-house in Lerwick for the three nights from
Thursday to Sunday, when I was due to proceed to Yell.
He had his own light-weight bike with him, on which he
had travelled over a large part of the European continent
and on which in the following year he cycled through
North Africa: we had not yet learned to distrust the
activities of Hitler's young followers. Our kind landlady
lent me her bike, a good but very heavy machine, and on
the Saturday we cycled down to Sumburgh and back on
the rough, waterbound and badly graded roads. To make
matters worse, I was under some pressure of time, as I
hoped to get back to Lerwick in time to send a letter off
with the *St Sunniva* when she sailed at (or after) 5 p.m. I
clearly recall my flagging efforts and the state of near-
exhaustion in which I reached Lerwick — and all in vain,
for as we came in to the town there was the *St Sunniva*
heading out of the harbour. The other gruelling
experience with a bicycle was in Yell, curiously enough in
the same year, about a month later. A friend and I
borrowed bikes to cycle north from Mid Yell and explore
as far as Gloup, where I had not yet been. The machine I
had was the property of the local policeman. He was a
very tall man, so the bike had rather a long stretch for my

legs and it had a back-peddling brake. I had difficulty in controlling the machine with any comfort and was rather apt, when climbing hills, to back-peddle unintentionally, whereupon the bike stopped and I fell off.

Since World War II, the coming of the oil-related activities and the introduction of vehicle ferries have led to a transformation of Shetland's roads. Here and there on a side road — though even they are mostly tarred now — one can still get some idea of what the old roads were like. The best (or worst) example I recall seeing recently of the old unimproved surface is on the road leading from the head of Basta Voe direct to Cullivoe, which has been downgraded in status in favour of the route via Gutcher, which connects with the ferry to Unst and Fetlar. Initially as traffic expanded burdens were imposed on the roads for which they had not been designed, and the deterioration was appalling, as roads crumbled away into the peat-moss. However, more recently there has been an enormous reconstruction programme, and the result, candidly, has been to provide roads far more splendid than the traffic justifies. At their best they are superb, in engineering, in surface and in a breadth more than adequate for the still relatively moderate traffic. There has been a good deal of realignment and straightening of bends and the outcome has been the experience of driving effortlessly at speeds three or four times what would have been possible fifty years ago. Of course in the process of reconstruction there were intermediate phases, when there were stretches of rough rubble. From one year to the next there were startling transformations: stretches which had been barely passable one summer were of near-motorway standard the next. In some stretches the road-makers, not content with reconstructing old roads or following the old lines, broke away to completely new routes. This could be disconcerting, for one found that the road no longer passed places one expected to see or even houses one intended to visit. But to anyone who remembers the old untarred tracks it is all barely credible. The road that is most disappointing is the busy one from Sumburgh Airport to Lerwick. A few miles south from Lerwick have been brought up to the standard of the best Shetland roads, but the rest is far below the standard of the best roads in Yell, which carry incomparably less traffic.

However, apart from the trunk routes, there are plenty of roads which, though now well surfaced, are still narrow and tortuous and give the impression of running through an endless desert of uninhabited moor. They do make one realise how little of the land surface of Shetland is used for any purpose except pasturing sheep. It is really rather a joy to get on to some of those rambling single-track roads, because they give a sense of liberation. As they attract fewer users, even in the tourist season, than the main routes to and from Sumburgh in one direction and Sullom Voe and Toft (for the North Isles ferries) in the other, there is little traffic by southern standards. Especially on the west side, in the area extending from Weisdale to Sandness, there is a maze of little roads linking isolated houses and settlements and giving glimpses of some entrancing coastal scenery. A motorist who wanders aimlessly round them will not be wasting his time. There need be no nervousness about venturing on to the narrower roads. The standard of manners among drivers is on the whole still high, and it results in a kind of competition in civility, when two drivers both stop at passing-places and each tries to entice the other to come on. Besides, the traffic is hardly ever heavy and generally it can only be described as absurdly light. It is true that driving on constantly twisting roads demands steady attention and can be tiring, but then one is never driving great distances.

Anyone touring in Shetland should remember that he will add enormously to his pleasure and comfort if he takes some picnic gear with him, perhaps a gas stove, some simple food and the wherewithal to make tea and coffee — including, not least important, a supply of drinking water. Owing to the peaty nature of the soil, one need not expect to find everywhere in Shetland the sparklingly fresh and clear streams familiar in the Scottish Highlands, though there are clear-running burns in Fetlar and Northmavine. But be warned: the old tradition of hospitality to wayfarers still survives, and if you ask at a house to have your water-container filled you must be prepared to decline politely an offer of a cup of tea.

People who do not know the islands often wonder whether it is worth their while to take their own cars when they go there on holiday. Until May 1983 my answer to that question would have been an emphatic 'Yes', but the experience which I shared with others at that time caused me to have second thoughts. I had booked to travel north with my car on the *St Clair* on Monday, 9th May. Just over a week before the sailing date I received a telephone message from P&O Ferries intimating somewhat brusquely and entirely without apology that the *St Clair* would be 'going to Sweden'. I was told that my car would be taken north on the *St Magnus* but I would go by plane on the Monday night, which meant that I would arrive in Lerwick with no overnight accommodation and no transport until my car arrived on the Tuesday morning. I protested that I was thus going to incur not only inconvenience but considerable and unexpected expense for an extra night's accommodation and for transport between Lerwick and my hotel, but this objection was shrugged off. It turned out that some passengers (selected how?) were privileged to travel on the *St Magnus*, though one couple who did so did not even have a car with them. No one who had this experience of finding the ship thus diverted from her normal run at the whim of the management will readily recover confidence in the sea-crossing. When we were in the plane between Dyce and Sumburgh on the Monday evening the Captain remarked to us pointedly that he hoped what had happened would encourage us to use the plane in future. If P&O Ferries were to decide to abandon the passenger trade, the plan of conveying cars by sea and their owners by air might become the pattern; but no one could claim it would have the convenience of accompanying one's own car from port to port. My hesitation about recommending the *St Clair* was reinforced on my southward trip a week later, after she had returned from her trip to Sweden (when she had acted as a 'Football Special' for an international match), because I had the unprecedented experience of being relegated to a berth in an inside cabin, although I had made my reservation two months before and I could see that the ship was only lightly booked.

The lightness of the traffic on Shetland roads does not arise from any dearth of cars — far from it. I do not know what the statistics may be, but it seems that the majority of households now have a vehicle of some kind. One becomes aware of the numbers of cars there are on occasions like a regatta, and I think the worst congestion I ever saw was at Aith on what seemed to be a Lifeboat Day. And it was impressive to survey the serried ranks of cars at the pier-head at Ulsta, left by the men and women who crossed Yell Sound daily for their employment in connection with the developments at Sullom Voe. But, that apart, there is nothing like the amount of daily movement, to and from work, that there is in the south. True, the 'rush hour' in and out of Lerwick is perceptible, but I have driven the eight miles from Burravoe to Mid Yell between nine and ten in the morning and met exactly one other vehicle, an experience one could hardly parallel elsewhere. There may be more movement at weekends. One Friday evening in June two or three years ago I happened to be at the ferry pier at Oddsta, in Fetlar, when some children who were at school in Lerwick were expected home for the weekend. There were eight cars on the pier that evening — on an island with only about seven miles of main road and a population below a hundred. Incidentally, for a time that same ferry terminal demonstrated one of the marvels of modern science. When the vehicle ferry started, Fetlar had no mains electricity and consequently no power to operate the ramps which have to be adjusted according to the rise and fall of the tide. But power for the ramp was then originated by remote control from the bridge of the ferry-boat. A short time before the boat reached the pier, one heard the generator starting up in preparation for her arrival. This was a touch of what seemed little short of magic, in a community where the source of so much power for heating and cooking is still found in what is brought out, by human labour, from the peak-banks.

The vast amount of road construction has not been carried out without much loss of amenity. Great masses of the peat in which Shetland is so rich and which supports the vegetation have been ripped off, to expose the rocks below. In a country where the soil is poor and growth slow it takes a long time for the scars to be effaced, though in some of the recent work there has been more care with reinstatement and re-seeding, with good results. More serious, and more enduring, are the results of the enormous amount of quarrying for road metal. True, in every part of the Scottish countryside one will find quite conspicuous quarry-holes by the roadside (which so often provide useful shelters for motorists picnicking or even camping for a night), but nowhere do the quarries seem so bald, baked and unashamed as they are in Shetland. Thanks to the devastating power of modern machinery, some terrible things have been done. Scalloway is one case in point. When seen from the classic viewpoint at the Scord, on the road coming over the hill from Lerwick, Scalloway is still dominated, as it has been for nearly four centuries, by Earl Patrick's castle, and when one gets down into the village, although a tasteless clutter of buildings adjacent to the castle interferes with a closer

view, some recent clearance has made it easier than it was
to see the building satisfactorily from the south and east.
But it is not so pleasant to approach Scalloway along the
Tingwall Valley. This is in some sense the most historic
track in Shetland, representing the route by which so
many men from the south and west of Shetland must have
made their way, after leaving their boats at Scalloway, to
the meeting of the *thing* or assembly at Tingwall Loch,
under the shadow of Shetland's principal church. Yet
now, almost at the same moment as you catch your first
glimpse of the top of the castle you are confronted by an
enormous quarry, a great gash in the hillside, with huge
machinery in it. It is interesting to anyone who wants to
know what Shetland is like beneath the surface, but has
no other appeal. The worst damage of all has been done
at the Mavis Grind, where half a hillside has been blasted
and bulldozed out of existence. I once alluded to this at a
debate in the National Trust about the supposed damage
being done to Ben Lawers through the encouragement
given to the public to climb that mountain (which is
surely the place in Scotland where it is easiest to attain an
altitude of 4000 feet — well, 3984); I remarked that,
given the comparative scales of the Lochtayside landscape
and the Shetland landscape, the damage done at the
Mavis Grind was as if about a third of Ben Lawers had
been simply obliterated, and that only those with no sense
of proportion could complain about the effects on mighty
Ben Lawers of the scratching and scraping of human feet.
In May 1983, when my niece and her husband returned
to Lerwick from their first drive to Hillswick, I found that
they had simply been unaware of crossing the Mavis
Grind, so completely has its character been effaced. It is
hard to credit that any local authority can be so
insensitive as the Shetland Islands Council has been in
authorising such large-scale devastation at one of the most
striking physical features within its jurisdiction.

3 ≡ *Pleasures Afloat:*
'The Eela' and 'The Banks'

'Hanging around harbour-sides', wrote Stevenson, 'is the richest form of idling', and someone else praised the joys of 'messing about in boats'. The first of those pleasures goes as far back for me as my memory does, for visits to Leith Docks and Granton Harbour with my father must have started almost as soon as I was able to walk the distance. Indeed it is more than likely that I first went in a pram. The second of those pleasures — the small boat — could hardly have begun quite as early, but it certainly goes back nearly as far as my memory is specific. Whether I was ever in a small boat before I was in Shetland for the first time in 1921 I could not say. If I was, it may quite possibly have been on highly contrasting water, the Union Canal in Edinburgh, where the boat-hirer was an old friend of my father, and in our household 'Johnnie Johnston' and 'the Canal' were synonymous. For many years, indeed as late as the 1940s, I occasionally pottered about on the Canal, and I might have been there oftener if Johnnie would have allowed me to pay for the hires, but he never would. Usually it was a matter of rowing, but I may be one of the last survivors of those who had the experience of travelling on the canal in a traditional horse-drawn barge. Johnnie's idea of a party was to assemble his friends on one of the workaday barges (spruced up for the occasion and furnished with a piano and picnic equipment) and take them up to Ratho. On one much later visit I rowed as far as that, and camped on the bank overnight. But I must confess that after I had become habituated to rowing in open water and holding a

E

steady course by observation over the stern I found the
incessant windings of the canal very trying.

The first small-boat expedition in Shetland,
mentioned in chapter 1, was to Orfasay in 1921. I do not
recall being off in a small boat in 1922, when my cousin
Magnie was not at home, and my father, much as he liked
being afloat, was a poor hand at managing a boat and
would not, I think, have been allowed to take a boat out
by himself. If my own skills in that department are
inherited, they must come from an earlier generation. I
do not remember a time when I was unable to row, and
although in later years I taught countless boys to row I
have no recollection of ever receiving any instruction
myself. This suggests that familiarity with boats and their
ways goes back to very early years. Curiously enough, my
first conscious memory of making frequent use of boats
belongs to the years between 1922 and 1929, when I was
not in Shetland but had holidays at various other places
by the sea, especially Rothesay and Dunoon but also
Anstruther in Fife. I first remember rowing on my own in
those Clyde resorts and it must have been in such a tame
environment that I first became used to that pleasure. In
the childish excitement of meeting the wake of the turbine
steamers as they tore past, I at least learned to keep a
boat's head on to approaching waves. At some stage now
indefinable, the use of a boat became for me an indispensable element in a holiday. And — significant fact
— all our holidays were 'at the seaside'; we never went to
inland resorts.

My earlier days in South Yell from 1929 onwards did
not offer any boating apart from fishing, for one could
hardly expect the local crofters to go out for pleasure and I
had no one else to join me, but on visits to Mid Yell I was
more fortunate, for with other young people I began an
investigation of the shores and surroundings of Mid Yell
Voe, which I was to continue later. There was that
remarkable little island Kay Holm, which contains that

rarity in Shetland, a cave accessible from the land, but it is really a sea-cave of which the entrance has collapsed, and after one has crawled through the low entrance a step or two takes one to water. There was that shapely cave on the north side of the entrance to the voe, popularly known as 'Dreepie-Nose' from the drip of water at the entrance, which though narrow could be penetrated for quite a distance if one stood up in the boat and used an oar as a paddle or a fending-pole. And, a little farther off, one could land on Hascosay, which deserves closer investigation than I have ever given it.

Oddly enough, in those early years I had some pleasure-boating in Lerwick, a thing which has been almost unknown in more recent times. The temptation of those beautiful boats lying so accessibly beside the slips and lodberries must have been such that I plucked up courage to ask if I could hire one. To the eternal credit of the owner, I got not a hire but a free loan. Knowing how precious boats are to their owners, I must surely have looked a competent sort of chap. On more than one occasion I was along the shore to the Knab, where I took some photographs, and on one expedition, probably in 1931, I got down the Bressay side, well on for the lighthouse. While no doubt I was handy enough with a pair of oars by that time, I knew nothing in those days about tides, but I realise now why it was so easy to go south and that what seemed a harder task on the way back was my first experience of an adverse tide.

My first sea-fishing expedition in Shetland was at Westsandwick in 1929. In the morning we gathered bait by going down to the beach with the ebb and drawing old sickles through the sand to catch sand-eels. Then we spent a happy afternoon with handlines along the cliffs as far as the Birrier and the Sweinna Stack, with a catch of 2½ score of haddock.

Fishing for haddock had the advantage of being carried on in deep water off cliffs, so that one could

combine the fishing with an inspection of the cliffs, and
on a later occasion, when handline-fishing from Strand in
Fetlar, I was shown the notable rock-formations on the
west side of the Wick of Gruting. From Gossabrough I
once fished for saithe on a summer day off the Ness, and
from the same place I once 'fished for gannets'. That was
another matter. In the food scarcity at the end of the War,
almost anything edible was marketable, and London
restaurants accepted 'Shetland goose', which was the
gannet. Consequently, there was for a time quite a trade
in those birds. The technique, I discovered (this was in
1945, two months or so after the end of the war in
Europe), was to shoot the birds from the cliffs and then go
round in the boat to collect the carcasses. This we did.
Fortunately, this particular sport did not have a long life.

The fishing I engaged in most was in a different type
of water, in relatively shallow tidal streams and not off
cliffs, and it took place evening by evening over many
summers — a form of what would now be called sea-
angling and known as 'the Eela'. This was fishing for
young saithe (sillocks in their first year, piltocks in their
second). The practice was to set out an hour or two before
sunset and come back an hour or two after sunset, the
boats working away while the sun went down behind the
north-west Mainland and made Roeness Hill indeed the
'Blew Mountain' which it is called on an early map. The
moon might be well up and the stars bright before we
were home. It was well known that the fish were more
plentiful, or at any rate more ready to 'take', in a tideway
or in the broken water of a tide-rip, and in South Yell our
fishing grounds were around the little island of Orfasay,
on the fringe of the tremendous tide-race of Yell Sound.
One man, at the oars, 'aandoed', that is, rowed with little
more effort than was necessary to keep the boat's head to
the tide while flies streamed out astern. Another man
lifted a thwart ('taft') and placed it across the quarters of
the boat, giving him a high perch from which to manage

two rods ('waands'), perferably of pitch-pine, which had the advantage of being less pliable than the bamboo which was sometimes used. Another fisher might manage another two waands from a taft behind him. The tackle consisted of six hooks, each with a fly. The preferred fly or 'busk' was 'hoe-tail', the fibrous structure of a dogfish tail from which the flesh had decayed and which glistened in the water, but white feathers were sometimes used. The cast of six hooks with their flies was carefully folded up when dry and was commonly wrapped in a scrap of newspaper and carried under the owner's cap until the time came to 'bend on' or attach it to the line on the 'waand'. The length of line was such that when the rod was raised upright in one hand the fish on the hooks came conveniently into the other hand, by which they could usually be shaken off to fall into the bottom of the boat. If the fish were taking well, one might have to lift four or more piltocks at once.

Often three or four boats or more might be working within hailing distance of each other, with a certain amount of badinage passing between them and some exchange — sometimes rather reserved — of information about the catch. 'We're gotten a good diet' was one remark that sticks in my mind. In the 1930s catches were reckoned by the score, and from five to ten score was usually considered fair. It was said, as the fishing dwindled, that at one time the catch had been reckoned by the 'kishie' or basket, then in scores and latterly in single fish. When the trip was over, the fish were divided among the men who had taken part in the expedition. It was a sport with its own rare character, but the object was not sport, for the piltocks, apart from a few fried when fresh, were salted and sun-cured for winter use.

Returning from the Eela late in the season, as the light faded, there might, before we reached the shore, be no more light than sufficient to distinguish land from sky, and then one had to use meads or sea-marks — not, of course, ahead, but astern, as all would be rowing and their eyes astern and not ahead. By the time we reached the banks it was just about pitch dark, and on a very calm evening, with the land reflected in the water, it might be extremely difficult, even for the most practised, to discern any features on the shore, or even to detect where water ended and land began. If the womenfolk came down, as they often did, with kishies to carry home the catch, they sometimes brought a 'blinkie' or electric torch to signal the position of the 'noost' where the boats were drawn up.

One of the noosts from which we set out and to which we returned involved walking along the edge of the sea-water loch of Galtagarth, and we frequently waded through the shallow water. Returning in the darkness, one's boots stirred up the 'mareel' or phosphorescence, and each step liberated what looked like a shower of diamonds. The amazing, the startling, beauty of the 'mareel' is a joy which I suspect many have never experienced. Besides having it on these returns from the Eela, one used to look over the stern of a steamer on a dark night and see how the screw churned up a fiery trail. This was a thing which, after long taking for granted, I had really forgotten about because I had not experienced it for years. Then one evening in Benderloch, when I had rowed across a tidal inlet to visit friends and returned much later than I had intended, the light had gone so completely that I was just able to distinguish land from sky. I suddenly found to my delight that as soon as I put my oars into the water they cascaded diamonds with every stroke. I believe it was one of the best displays I have ever seen, and I never succeeded in equalling it again on succeeding nights, though to all appearances conditions were the same.

The other sport that provided an occasional occupation, far less regularly than the Eela, was the mackerel fishing. The tackle used was suitable for the most favourable conditions — a line of about three dozen hooks and flies, which might either be tried near the surface or sunk well down in the water. If there were any signs of shoals around, either from the broken water they caused by playing on the surface or from the oily film they left on the water, boats would go out. But mackerel are a chancy fish, and the movements of their shoals unpredictable, so that one boat might do well and another nearby might be blank.

A boat was possibly the most costly piece of equipment the average Shetlander possessed in the days before mechanical transport, and from that point of view alone it required careful attention. The loving treatment which boats received resulted in their having long lives: fifty years was not out of the ordinary, and after such a space of time a well-maintained boat might still be in excellent order. The prevailing practice was to draw boats up on a beach when not in use, though in places where there was really sheltered water and a good depth close inshore they were kept lying off, sometimes on a running line. If one happened to be going ashore for a short time between trips, there was an ingenious trick which made it possible to keep a boat afloat even on an ebbing tide. A stone attached by a rope to the stern was balanced on the 'honeyspot' where the gunwales came together at the stern. Then, holding a longer rope, attached to the bow, one pushed the boat off the shore as forcefully as possible. When she ran out to the extent of the bow rope she might stop with a jerk sufficient to topple the stone into the water, and, failing that, a sharp tug on the bow rope might do the trick — but it might not. The whole business was a matter of a careful balance of forces and if the stone was too delicately poised and there was any movement in the water it might topple over the side before the bow rope ran fully out. Then one just had to try again — and again.

When drawn up, the boat was kept firmly on her keel by shoring her up with three large stones on each side,

carefully placed to correspond to the positions of the three
ribs. Shetlanders were well aware of the simple fact,
which I have so often had to mention to people fooling
around in a boat on a beach, that a boat is built to
withstand pressure from outside rather than from inside.
A sturdy piece of wood could be used in place of a stone to
shore her up, and a very careful owner would sometimes
insert a piece of wood or even a piece of leather between a
stone and the planking, to protect the latter's paint or
surface. Then she would be tied by ropes to boulders fore
and aft, at least if any wind was expected. When a boat
was secured for the winter, in her winter 'noost', which
might be hollowed out of a grassy bank above the beach,
extra precautions were taken. Everyone knew only too
well how readily a boat could be lifted by a gale and
smashed to pieces, and I had direct knowledge of three
such occurrences.

How easy or how difficult it might be to draw a boat
up and down between the water and her noost depended
very much on what kind of beach it was. Sand or soft
shingle is the worst, large boulders are not too easy; a
pebbly beach is best, for the iron-shod keel slides fairly
easily on pebbles. However, the process was facilitated by
the use of 'linns' or skids. Most commonly these were
pieces of driftwood, but the traditional linns were the ribs
of the 'caain' whales' which had so commonly been cast
up on Shetland beaches in earlier days; these became
polished by use, and were marvellously effective. It need
not be said that it was always much easier to get a boat
down from the noost to the sea than to draw her up, and I
found that I could generally manage to get my own boat
down single-handed, by more or less 'cradling' the stem
in my arms and pushing. The knack in drawing a boat
up, especially without 'linns', is to lift as well as pull.
Piltack waands, normally left in the boat or at her side in
the fishing season, found their winter resting place at the
gable of the house, where the remains of whales were

again handy, for a couple of whale vertebrae, knocked into the interstices between stones in the wall, formed excellent brackets.

Superstitions connected with fishing, many of which have been recorded from earlier days, were well remembered and often alluded to in my time, but probably few of them were any longer taken seriously: I was often told that 'the old men' would never have done such and such. Possibly taboos were often observed rather by way of keeping up old customs than because of any belief in their efficacy. I would never allow anyone to whistle in a boat, for fear of raising the wind (a belief not peculiar to Shetland), and to mention a cat on a fishing expedition would be unthinkable. I would not worry so much about the taboo on references to a minister (which, I believe, arose from the fact that the minister, like the cat, was greedy for the fish to which he used to be entitled as part of the teinds or tithes in his stipend). I still feel seriously about one point, and I suspect there are many more who would never dream of turning a boat other than 'sungaets' or clock-wise when setting out from the shore — though, to be fair, a right-handed man will naturally prefer to pull his right-hand oar.

The use of a boat for exploration and for travel from place to place is something I shall have more to say about in the next chapter, when I recount my adventures with my own boat and its outboard motor, but of course, even if one had reached an interesting stretch of coast with the help of the outboard, closer investigation of the various features of 'the banks' was a matter for manoeuvring with the oars. There were arches and tunnels (like the one in the White Hill of Gossabrough) which one could 'motor' through with perfect safety, but it was preferable to relish them in a more leisurely way. I happen to have notes, made at the time, of an outing to part of the Yell coast in 1948. At that stage I no longer had my own boat, but an obliging friend in Houlland (between Burravoe and

Hamnavoe) lent me his, and with some companions I
rowed round to the cliffs on the south-east coast of Yell.
These cliffs are not conspicuous for their height, as their
highest point barely reaches 300 feet above the sea. Yet,
unlike some higher cliffs, they are at many points quite
perpendicular and fall directly into water which, only a
few yards from the shore, is 30-40 fathoms deep. They are
impressive when viewed from the sea and, like most of the
Shetland coast, they are the haunt of myriads of sea-
birds. As the coast faces the open North Sea calm and
settled conditions are essential if the cliffs are to be seen in
safety and comfort.

On this 1948 visit, early in August, the sea was
ideally calm, with a rise and fall of only a few inches on
the cliff face. Half an hour's rowing round the low-lying
Heoganess brought us past the 'Windy Clett' ('Stanyard
Rock' on the chart), a conspicuous rock which marks the
extreme south-east corner of Yell. Here Heoganess
narrows to an isthmus only a few yards in breadth,
separating the head of Burra Voe from the sea. Once
(with some assistance) I drew my boat across that isthmus
to avoid the exposed water at the back of Heoganess. The
view of the cliffs from the shore at this point is very fine
and evoked one of the few complimentary remarks made
about Yell: a nineteenth-century writer described the spot
as 'more beautifully diversified and grand than anything I
have seen elsewhere in Shetland'. From the low-lying
isthmus the cliffs rise within the space of two or three
hundred yards to a height of nearly 300 feet above
Ramnagio, the highest they attain anywhere on the east
side of Yell, and continue with a similar height round a
broad bay which terminates in the mass of rock known as
the Horse of Burravoe.

On this occasion there was an unexpected obstacle to
our further progress, for a basking shark was feeding off
the next point of rock we had to round. These monsters
are not uncommon in Shetland in the summer months,

expecially where they find deep water near cliffs. I once saw one (and indeed was photographed standing on it) which had stranded and died in the shallow waters of Westsandwick Voe, and its length was about 28 feet. The present specimen seemed to be a large one. As it slowly circled round, it raised and lowered the dorsal fin, almost like the sail of a small boat — a feature which causes the creature to be known sometimes as a sailfish. The tip of the tail was nearly always visible, and the snout seemed to come up each time the mouth opened. The whole display was a very fair impression of the traditional sea-serpent. While basking sharks rarely attack boats, and are considered harmless unless they are interfered with, they do not, like whales, show any nervousness at the approach of a boat, and they are usually treated with respect. The other members of the party went ashore for a bit while I quietly worked the boat round between the shark and the rocks. After the others rejoined me and we went on to explore the cliffs we glanced back occasionally towards the shark, which long continued to cruise around the same patch of water.

When the cliffs first rise to the heights of Ramnagio they form a semi-circular recess called the Ladies' Hole. They are steep, but a good many patches of grass are interspersed among the black rocks and there are ledges which afford nesting-places for fulmars ('maalies' in Shetland) and puffins ('tammy-nories'). The fulmars glide and soar in their effortless flight, aided by the air currents set up by even the lightest breeze among the cliffs. With their rather stiff, sturdy wings, they resemble a man-made plane perhaps more than any other bird does, and when they come over the water, at low level, towards a boat, they look like fighter planes coming in to attack. A large number of fulmar nestlings, in their ample grey and white down, are on ledges, often just beneath an overhanging cliff top, which are out of reach but can be seen at close quarters from adjacent points. In August each chick is well grown, but still a mass of fluff which never stirs from the nest. It is sometimes possible to be near enough to rouse them to their unpleasant habit of ejecting a stream of foul fluid from their mouths and yet not be within reach of it. The puffins take to the sea at our approach and sit on the water some way off. A pointed stack, or detached part of the cliffs, is occupied by shags ('scarfs'), who sit on each jagged peak. A few black guillemots ('tysties') are about, always throwing up their heels and diving at our approach.

A little to the north, in a cliff which the map calls White Hamar, is the finest cave in this part of the coast, sometimes known as the Blue Hole. As we entered the cave, we could see a violent disturbance in the otherwise still water. Before we could speculate on the cause, a thickly packed shoal of mackerel dashed past, under and around the boat. Inside the cave, the lofty, high-pitched roof and walls have the colourings which it is always so astonishing to find in a sea-cave — vivid reds, greens and purples, besides brown, black and grey. Sea-urchins ('scadman's heids'), their colour ranging from almost white, through pink, to red, are on the walls, here and there exposed by the ebbing tide but mostly far beneath the surface of the clear water. On ledges many shags, and well-grown young, are nesting. With their nests often only a few feet above high-water mark, their dark green plumage is a good camouflage against black and green rocks. The birds' most conspicuous feature, against this background, is their dark yellow bills, but they usually reveal their presence, when alarmed, by loudly uttering their hoarse croaks from outstretched heads. The cry of the shag, echoing from the dark recesses of a cave, sounds more like the bark of an animal than the sound of any bird. As the boat approached, the adults invariably craned their long necks and turned their heads from side to side. Some made off with little hesitation, to flop into the sea and either dive under the boat or flap noisily along the surface towards the entrance, while others, though in a growing state of alarm, held their ground. One bird, more tenacious than all the rest, remained on the nest while the boat came alongside the rocks beneath it. When I stood up the shag and I were within a few feet of each other. In its growing excitement, the bird's cry became more and more highly pitched, almost resembling a yelp or brief 'yowl', as from a cat. Each squawk was accompanied by a vigorous shake of the outstretched head. Indignation could not have been more plainly expressed. The birds which made a steep descent into the water between the rocks and the boat reached the surface clumsily. Normally, given plenty of space, the bird settled down gently by the stern, but I could see that with a sharper descent, as the feet struck the water first, the body tilted forward and the breast entered the water with a resounding splash. Then diving, and swimming under the boat, the birds made out to sea to congregate on the water or on outlying rocks. A warning: when entering a cave or traversing a tunnel and arousing birds to fly off overhead, it is not a bad plan to drape an old raincoat over one's head.

As we were leaving the cave, the mackerel rushed in again, as if they had been waiting for us to vacate their place of refuge. We wondered if they had been sheltering from the basking shark.

In the angle of the cliffs before the Horse of Burravoe is reached there are two more gios. One, with sloping, grassy banks and a narrow entrance, is the home of many puffins. Another has perpendicular or overhanging walls of red rock. Lying off it are two stacks. From seaward they looked small in comparison with the cliffs, but as we passed behind them they were quite impressive.

The Horse itself is a huge bastion, 100 to 200 feet in height, jutting nearly a quarter of a mile out to sea, with almost perpendicular walls and throwing off buttresses on each side. It is one of the most prominent landmarks — or sea-marks — on the east side of Shetland, visible from long distances and unmistakeable with its characteristic shape, whether seen from north or south. Along the south side of the Horse are more gios and caves, and most of the rock is red. At one point the sea penetrates from side to side of a mass of rock, but only through a narrow cleft. We explored a cave with a low, narrow entrance. It extends far into the rock, but the rather shallow bottom, strewn with large boulders, made it impossible to reach the extremity. Immediately to the east, as we proceeded along the south side of the Horse, is a natural arch through one of the buttresses. It is quite high, but too narrow to row through. On previous visits there had been too much swell for it to be safe to take a boat through at all, but on this occasion it was possible to do so. On the further, outer side, the ledges above and around the arch form a most beautiful nesting place for a colony of kittiwakes.

The Horse terminates in the 'Stack of the Horse', beyond a low and narrow isthmus. On the north side there are a couple of good arches in a buttress. Half a mile or so farther north, the White Hill of Gossabrough has a natural tunnel which is easy to traverse — quite wide and high, and with deep water except at one point where care may be required. It is said that a boat once entered this tunnel with her mast stepped, but when the swell lifted her the mast struck the roof and went through the bottom of the boat.

On our return trip we made a straight course across the bay south of the Horse, carrying us far outside the water where we had seen the shark at work. That expedition was one on which, as I said, I made notes at the time and indeed contributed a 'Nature Note' to *The Scotsman,* but much the same (apart from the basking shark) could be reported of many occasions, and a trip round those particular 'high banks' was a regular treat for visiting friends, summer after summer.

4 ≣ My Best Thirty Pounds Worth

I must have realised from an early stage that the pleasure of holidaying in Shetland would be multiplied by the availability of a boat. I may have been influenced by reading J. R. Tudor's *The Orkneys and Shetland* (1883) and learning how that enterprising man had hired boats to explore spectacular pieces of coastline. But it was easy to see that nineteenth-century tourists had obtained the use of boats more readily than would be possible in the twentieth century, for there was a bigger population then and more men ready to earn a shilling or two by putting themselves and their craft at the disposal of visitors. No one now, a century later, should imagine that he can follow the advice Tudor so casually gives: 'Engage a boat'. At the same time, there were any number of attractive coastal features which there was no hope of seeing by public transport. Even the little islands in Yell Sound, for example, have good cliff scenery. Viewed from Yell and the Mainland they look almost featureless scraps of detached land, but inspection at close quarters reveals that Lamba, Muckle Holm and Little Roe (with the red cliffs which entitle it to be called 'the red island') have an array of caves, tunnels and arches, making each a miniature of Eshaness or Graveland. Finally, my own initial experiences in borrowed boats had shown something of the pleasure the exploration of 'the banks' could afford.

But, while friends and even casual acquaintances were, with characteristic generosity and trust, ready enough to lend me a boat, it became obvious that, to use a Shetland proverb, 'It's guid tae hae freends but it's no guid tae pick oot their een'. If I was going to get as much boating as I craved, in the course of the long periods of two-three months I was now spending in Shetland, and if I was going to have freedom to explore on the water as I was already exploring by land, it would be necessary to imitate the MacNeils (was it?) who were not in the Ark with Noah because 'they had a boat of their own'. The direct stimulus came from a treasured friend the late W. D. Johnson, of Reafirth, Mid Yell, in whom I found a kindred spirit. Willie was in business as a hosiery merchant (and a very capable one), but he had recently had a small Shetland boat, of nine feet keel (about 15 feet overall) built for him by John Smith of Stivler, North-a-Voe. As he explained to me, he had never been much drawn to mechanical transport by land, and the idea of imitating the young fellows who even then often had motor-bikes did not make much appeal, so he decided to experiment with outboard motors. When, at the second attempt, he found a suitable model, this provided his recreation on fine summer evenings and on the afternoon of each Wednesday, which he usually treated as a half-day.

As I discovered so well over the years when I have had a boat — successive boats — of my own, the management of even a small boat calls for a 'confederate'. To begin with, one needs help to draw the boat up on a beach, if not to draw her down. Then one may like to be relieved for a spell at the oars or tiller. Besides, a confederate makes useful ballast, moveable at a word of command. A Shetland boat, with its pointed stern, is not well suited to an outboard, for both the weight of the motor and the pull of the screw tend to draw the boat down aft, as would not happen in a boat with a square stern or full quarters, a boat 'with something to sit on aft'. The first time I started up my outboard without a

passenger and without ballast it was alarming to see the
boat rise before me 'like a barn door', as I put it, and
completely obscure my vision ahead. A passenger can sit
up forward and give a good fore-and-aft trim. Not only
so. A Shetland boat with an outboard, lacking the
steadying effect of oars or sails, can be very lively in
choppy or jumbly water, and if a passenger leaves his
thwart and seats himself on the floorboards ('tilfers') he
lowers the centre of gravity instead of constituting the
topweight which humans normally create in a small boat.
I owe a good deal to successive confederates over the
years.

At any rate, I became Willie Johnson's confederate.
It became almost a routine to walk over to Mid Yell on a
Wednesday morning, have a boating expedition in the
afternoon and either return to Hamnavoe that evening or
stay overnight. Willie — out of deference to the fears of
the women in the household — had adopted the technique
which I had used in my landward expeditions of never
advertising movements in advance, and it was with an air
of almost conspiratorial stealth that we set out for the
Broch of Burraness on the other side of Basta Voe, for
Urie in Fetlar (an enchanting spot on a beautiful evening)
or for a cruise round Hascosay. Though to be fair we did
not always decide on our destination until we were
already afloat.

I suppose that W. D. J. did more to shape my future
life than some academics have done, because ever since I
followed his example and acquired my own boat in 1933 I
have regarded the possession of a boat as one of the
essentials of a full life, and during more than thirty of the
years which have passed since then I have owned something that floats. If, in 1932, I was guilty of the sin of
covetousness, I can only repent, but the fact is that my
nineteen-year-old heart craved for a boat, which would
give me more pleasure than anything else in the world. So
in the winter of 1932-33 I commissioned Mr Smith to

F

build me another nine-footer, and I took delivery when I went north for my summer holiday in July 1933. The price for the craft, with four oars, all painted and complete, was — wait for it — £11. And some said, 'That's a fine boat you've got, but you paid too much for her. A pound a foot of keel is enough'. The £11 was certainly in one sense more than enough for a student who was living on two scholarships which together produced £70, plus another £20 or so earned by casual tutoring. My father, however, handsomely gave me £5 towards a purchase from which he (and my mother and sister) were to derive a good deal of pleasure in coming years. I saw little prospect of acquiring even a reconditioned outboard motor, but I had my twenty-first birthday in April 1934 and my present from my parents (who on the morning of my birthday gave me 'symbolic delivery' by presenting me with a toy motor-boat) was the major part of the £17.10s which a second-hand outboard cost. W. D. J.'s was an Elto Fisherman, mine a very similar Elto Lightweight and like his of 4 h.p. and with twin cylinders. The two cylinders were a great advantage. A lob of spray over the quarter (where most of the spray came aboard, as a Shetland boat is so designed as to keep very dry forward) sometimes shorted one cylinder, but the other would continue to drive the boat along at a low speed comfortable in broken water. All in all, I had fewer spots of bother with that motor than with any of the three I have owned since.

It might be hard to say which was the more important event, the acquisition of the boat or that of the outboard, and I have vivid memories of both. The boat of course was built at Mid Yell and had somehow to be transported to Hamnavoe, about 10½ miles by road and 12½ by sea. Nowadays I suppose the solution would be to put the boat on a lorry, but in those days that would never have occurred to anyone, and I doubt very much if there were any lorries in Yell in those days anyway. I suppose

we could have put the boat on board the *Earl*, but that
would have cost money which I could not afford and it was
never even suggested. The boat was too small to tow
behind the *Earl*, even at her eight knots or so, though I
recall just about that time seeing T. J. Spence, the landlord
of Burravoe, coming down from Mid Yell in tow astern of
the steamer, but his was a much longer boat than mine and
even so he had found it tricky to keep her from being
swamped over the quarters. In correspondence before I
went north that summer, W. D. J. had written of perhaps
giving me a tow with his boat 'as far as Gossabrough or on
towards the Horse', whence I could certainly have rowed
the remaining 4-5 miles. The question was still undeter-
mined when, on the afternoon of Saturday, 22nd July,
1933 (after arriving in Hamnavoe on the Friday) I went to
Mid Yell to take delivery. Willie and I crossed the voe in
his boat, to find my own awaiting me, fresh in the green
and white paint which I had chosen and which I always
adhered to thereafter, both in that boat and my second
Shetland boat. 'You're now the proud possessor of a small
boat', said Willie. We re-crossed the voe, each rowing his
own boat. The thrill then came closest to being paralleled
when, twenty years later, I took delivery at Connel Ferry
of my second boat (again a Shetland model). I recall saying
to my confederate on that occasion, 'Do you realise that
I'm afloat in my own boat for the first time since 1939?'

At some point on that memorable weekend in 1933
an unexpected solution was proposed for the transport of
my boat to Hamnavoe. At that time a motor vessel called
the *Innovator* was operating in the North Isles. She had
been introduced with a view to regular competition with
the *Earl*, but that phase had been short-lived and she was
by this time more or less 'tramping' as cargo offered. On
the Saturday she was lying at North-a-voe, where her
skipper lived, and we learned that she was due to go south
to Lerwick on the Monday. We learned sometime and
somehow. How the arrangement was made I have no

recollection, but it must have been by word of mouth, directly or indirectly, as there were no phones then in Yell. How well we managed without them. At any rate, I recall an early hour on a fine Monday morning, the voe lying calm and the first curls of reek just beginning to rise from one or two lums, when I rowed across from Reafirth to join the *Innovator*. I went on board and the new boat was towed astern. It was a most enjoyable trip, yarning in the wheelhouse of the motor vessel and picking up information about the rocks off the east side of Yell, including the position of the rock on which the *Islander*, another motor vessel which competed briefly with the *Earl*, had been wrecked the previous year. Hosea Moar, now skipper of the *Innovator*, had on that occasion been engineer on the *Islander* and suddenly saw a rock coming through her bottom. This was my first close acquaintance from seaward with a stretch of coast which was to become increasingly familiar to me in years to come on my trips up and down and on various excursions into the caves, arches and gios.

The *Innovator* came in between Greenholm and the Burgi Skerry, and there I was transferred to my own craft to row into Hamnavoe. As it was about an ebb, I knew I could not get up to the head of the voe, and made for the shore at the back of the Ness of Galtagarth, which remained my 'low-water station' for years. How far my arrival with the new boat that morning was expected I cannot say. There certainly had been no arrangements, for I had had no communication with Hamnavoe since I left on the Saturday, but — as happened so often — word did get around in the most amazing manner and I suspect half the parish knew that I had gone to Mid Yell to fetch my new boat. At any rate, a sharp-eyed friend, Geordie Hughson, had spied from his home at the Hillhead my transhipment from the *Innovator* and he was down on the shore to meet me — one of so many unexpected and unaffected acts of kindness which I experienced. He at once gave his verdict, 'A bonnie peerie ting o' a boat'.

Inevitably a new boat was a focus of interest and conversation, indeed gossip, and there were always those ready to criticise any flaws which might be detected or imagined. I recall a remark about a man (not in Yell) who — with that astonishing aptitude which characterises Shetlanders — had built a boat without any training or apprenticeship, and the judgment was, 'A. B. is a very clever chap, but he can't build a boat'. Even that boat, however, was serviceable, as I learned in practice. Any initial doubts about the merits of the one I had just acquired in 1933 were overcome when people experienced her: 'I think she pulls like a witch', said Johnnie Williamson the first time he and I rowed her from Hamnavoe to Burravoe. We were conveying a couple of sheep as well as Johnnie's dog, a creature which had a perfect passion for being afloat and when we drew the boat down to the water would always dash past us and take a flying leap aboard.

Later on in the day of my arrival, when the tide had risen, I moved the boat round from 'the back of the Ness' to what was to be her normal home — the 'Arisdale banks' to the west of the mouth of the Hamnavoe burn, where, in the distant days when the men in land-locked Arisdale, out of the sight of the sea, had boats, they had the noosts for their craft. Here I made a tactical error which speaks volumes for the standards of conduct in Shetland in those days. In my pride of possession, I had come north equipped with a chain and padlock with which I proposed to secure the oars. I never used the chain and padlock, for it was pointed out to me forcefully that it was contrary to all usage and 'They wouldn't like it', and I capitulated. It may be news to some readers that in those days even houses, never mind boats, were not locked (or rather 'keyed', in the local idiom). If the occupants were going to be absent for some hours, there was a convention of leaving the key in place outside the door, just to indicate that there was no one at home.

Another convention was that one should not knock before entering a friend's or neighbour's house: I have been rebuked, 'Gordon Donaldson, you surely know us well enough to come in without knocking at the door'. Goods of all kinds would be left unattended at the roadside, in perfect trust. The general atmosphere of security for property applied in Lerwick as well as in the country: for years after I began to use the Queen's Hotel, guests there did not have keys for their bedrooms. And the same was true of the ships. Not only did the earlier vessels not have locks on their cabin doors, but on some, perhaps all, of them there was no means at all of securing a cabin door from either inside or outside. Locking became usual on the third *St. Clair* after the oil developments began their malign influence, and on the present, fourth, *St. Clair* passengers are issued with keys as a matter of course. The deplorable change in morality is shown every week by the columns of offences now reported in *The Shetland Times*. The number of cases which came before the sheriff in Lerwick in 1953-54 was only 84; it was more than ten times as many — 894 — in 1977-78. Looking at this record, no one who thinks straight can possibly believe that crime is caused by poverty and not by affluence. By 1982, when prosperity had begun to recede, the figure dropped to 752.

While I was dissuaded from flaunting proprietorship over my boat by padlocking the oars, I did a good deal to make the noost my own. There was at that time only one other boat kept at that particular spot — indeed it was the only other boat belonging to any of the eleven houses of Hanmavoe, which at once gives the lie to the common assertion of inobservant visitors that 'every household has a boat' — and she was seldom used, so I had things all my own way. I carefully laid a row of of large stones down the beach, to make it easier for passengers (especially those without rubber boots) to embark dry-shod, and lined the stones up with a large, conspicuous and immovable boulder. This was sometimes a useful mark when coming ashore in the mirk on returning from the Eela, though the essential bearing was in fact over the stern, lining up an old house on the Copister skyline with the point of Fineback, which brought me into the noost.

However, besides the 'Arisdale banks' there was what I have already called my 'low-water station' at the back of the Ness of Galtagarth. This offered a fine clean, steep-sloping beach of small boulders, but, besides being less sheltered, was not very convenient of access. Getting to and from it involved a crossing of the 'brig' or stepping-stones where the Loch of Galtagarth discharged into the voe. The stones had been carefully laid at one time, but some of them had been upset, so it was said, by unneighbourly fishermen from Whalsay in search of mussels as bait — and had gone unpunished, unlike those guilty of a similar action in Earl Patrick's time, more than 300 years before, when men 'quha hes tane bait and brokin doun the brig of Strome' found themselves in trouble with the local magistrate. It was a precarious business crossing these stones, especially if one was carrying some gear, and when the water-level was really low it was better to ignore the 'brig' and wade through the shallow water alongside, running as it did into or out of the loch.

Obviously in 1933, that first season, when I had no means of propulsion except oars — 'the hand cycle' as I heard it called — I was much restricted and not very ambitious, hardly venturing beyond the waters I was already familiar with. I was out again and again in Hamna Voe and across it to visit friends in Copister, I had some evenings at the Eela, I began what was to become a habit of taking the boat along to Burravoe to shop and to meet the steamer, I explored the gios in Burraness and I was round the familiar little island of Orfasay. My farthest expeditions were very modest ones — to the head of Burra Voe on one side and the Broch of

Copister on the other, about 3 ¼ miles in each direction
from my base. In post-war years, when I no longer had a
boat of my own and sometimes borrowed one, I was more
than once to row as far as the Horse of Burravoe, but in
1933 I was still feeling my way, learning more about the
boat and more about the sea. I finished the season, at the
end of September, by painting the boat and rowing her
along to Burravoe, where the friendly merchant allowed
me to put her, for that winter and each successive winter,
in the barrel-store.

The 1934 season was my first with the outboard. The
motor went north (partly dismantled) as part of my
personal luggage, in a cabin trunk. It was not, I think, on
that occasion that a man handling my baggage on the *St.
Sunniva* asked, 'Is it coals you have in there?', for the
explanation of the weight was usually the books and
portable typewriter which regularly went north with me.
Certain advance preparations had to be made before I
began the more ambitious boating I now envisaged. I had
to learn not only about the farther waters in which I now
hoped to venture — and for this I equipped myself with a
chart — and about how the boat would behave with the
outboard, but even about the mechanism of the outboard
itself. I was as yet incredibly ignorant of internal
combustion engines, and hardly knew a sparking-plug
from a carburettor. I recall, not many years before, when
a more mechanically-minded school-fellow was speaking
knowledgeably about cubic capacity, I thought he meant
the capacity of the fuel tank. But then I had spent my
early years in a milieu where motor cars were still such a
comparative rarity that one might hear the remark (in
Edinburgh), 'I see a motor at so-and-so's door; they must
have had to call the doctor'. When my outboard had been
delivered to me in Edinburgh I felt I should make sure
that it was in perfect working order before taking it north.
I arranged with a friend — a Shetlander, W. J. M.
('Sonny') Moar — to take me and it down to his rowing

club at Portobello one evening to try it out. The machine turned out to be in perfect order: my only initial trouble was that in my ignorance I was unaware that it was not only unnecessary, but positively disastrous, to flood the carburettor when starting hot, and I wasted a lot of time in my earlier runs in Shetland on that account.

The boat had to be adapted to take the outboard. Various devices have been used by other owners of Shetland boats — a bracket out beyond the 'horn' at the extremity of the stern, which increased the back-weight and made it more awkward to reach the motor if it needed attention; a bracket over the quarter; or a 'trunk' or box through which the driving shaft entered the water, but this had the disadvantage that the motor was unable to tilt if the propeller met an obstacle. Following Willie Johnson's example, I took the simplest and most drastic plan of having a piece cut off the stern; but I hit on the idea of retaining the piece which had been removed so that it could be replaced with a couple of screws and butterfly nuts when the motor was not in use, to make it impossible to detect, except on very close inspection, that the boat had been modified. The resultant work, carried out to my design, was done by the late Bobby Robertson, then resident at Overby, Burravoe, a man with exceptional gifts of craftsmanship even by Shetland standards. So thoughtfully, he brought my altered boat alongside the *Earl* when I arrived in Burravoe on 6th July 1934. How well he judged my expectant frame of mind.

Just as 1933 had been experimental with the boat, so 1934 was more or less experimental with the outboard. I was not in fact the pioneer of outboard-motoring in South Yell, for Mr William Turnbull, of the Edinburgh auctioneering firm of Lyon and Turnbull, who owned the Burravoe estate from 1910 to 1923, had had an outboard — a model which belonged to the days before the starting-cord and was started, or not started, by a knob on the flywheel. His experiment had caused some unpleasant-

ness, for when he came along from Burra Voe to Hamna
Voe with his noisy contraption and found no trout in
waters which were usually well stocked, he blamed his
tenants for poaching — not necessarily entirely without
cause — while they blamed him for frightening the fish
away. However, when my motor arrived a good many
years had passed since Turnbull's effort, and the younger
generation, who did not remember it, were apt to regard
me as having introduced the outboard to South Yell. My
outboard was certainly the only one around, so whenever
the characteristic sound of that two-stroke engine was
heard — and it was heard for long distances in the quiet of
a Shetland evening, indeed all the way from Burravoe to
Hamnavoe, so they told me — everyone knew that
Gordon was on the sea.

One problem was a means of getting the outboard up
and down regularly between the barn beside the house
and the boat at her noost, for it was a long way to carry a
somewhat awkward piece of machinery weighing over
forty pounds. A wheelbarrow was sometimes used, not
very successfully, and then I got the use of the shed beside
the kirkyard dyke which had once been built for the
accommodation of the minister's mare (see chapter 6),
but even from that point it was quite a carry, across two
fences and the uneven uncultivated ground of the Wirlie.
The problem was solved only a year later, after my father
had made a box big enough to hold the outboard. It went
north, like the traditional seaman's 'kist', with our
personal baggage inside, and was then installed beside the
noost. This was padlocked, whether people liked it or not.

Yet another problem soon emerged, when I ventured
on the longer runs which I had in mind. The first new
ground I broke was a trip to Ulsta on the Monday after
my arrival, to collect a suitcase which had somehow been
left behind in Lerwick and had come north by the
overland route — once more one marvels at how we
learned that it had arrived in Ulsta, but we did. Even on

that trip I found that the half-gallon tank did not contain
enough fuel to carry us to Ulsta and back, and we had to
re-fuel off the Broch of Copister. It was worse a week
later, when we set out for Mid Yell. The tank, full, would
run for an hour (six miles or so), but if I had to re-fuel in
any swell I was lucky if I got it half-full, and frequent re-
fuelling was time-wasting and uncomfortable. That first
trip to Mid Yell took over three hours. Before the next
season I had a copper tank made which held a gallon and
a half, enough for about twenty miles non-stop running.
In 1934 I made no more long trips, but confined myself to
Hamnavoe, Burravoe, Copister, Orfasay and the Eela,
but even within that scope I found the boat an enormous
convenience as well as a source of pleasure. One
adventure was the use of my boat to lay the buoys for the
Burravoe regatta, of which I write in chapter 6. I totalled
nearly 150 miles in the season.

    In 1935, now with the new tank and the motor handy
in its box at the banks, I at once launched out on a more
ambitious programme. Two days after I got the boat out
of her winter home, rowed her along to Hamnavoe and
fitted the new tank, I set out for Mid Yell — this time
non-stop; in the evening Willie Johnson and I went out to
Burraness on the far side of Basta Voe; next day I
returned to Hamnavoe (in just under two hours), and, as
if I had not had enough, went to the Eela and round
Orfasay (rowing) at night. In the next fortnight I was four
times in Burravoe — shopping, visiting friends at Overby
and going alongside the steamer — and made my first
close exploration of the cliffs round the Horse which I
described in the previous chapter. These two or three
weeks in July 1935 may not have been typical, but it is
that kind of thing that sticks in my mind as if it had been a
pattern.

    However, I had plans for much more extended
cruising, and had arranged for the company of a
congenial confederate, Randal Stalker, a medical

student, whom I had met when on holiday in Arran in April; he was a mountaineer (which I never was) but was not loath to try sea-faring, and he came up to Shetland at the end of July. He had had a lot of camping experience, and he brought the necessary equipment for both of us, but as it turned out we rarely needed it. We set out on the last day of July for Fetlar. I first showed Randal round the Horse and then we struck across for the north-west corner of Fetlar, to thread our way through rock-strewn water and land briefly on the island of Daaey. We then carried on along the 'Blue Banks' of the north of Fetlar, past that remarkable lump of rock the Clett and into the Wick of Gruting, where I knew we would have hospitality from the Williamsons at Strand.

After a night at Strand we were off again, across to Unst. We knew we would find two friends from Edinburgh, Kitty and Annie Moar, having a holiday with their kinsfolk beside Muness Castle. When we arrived we found that they had been invited to go that afternoon to the island of Uyea to visit Major Neven-Spence (who in the following November became M.P. for Orkney and Shetland) and his family. True, I had met the Major and his wife previously, in Edinburgh, but it was characteristic of the egalitarian Shetland society that it was taken for granted that Randal and I would be welcome in Uyea along with Kitty and Annie. It was, of course, convenient for us to take them in my boat direct from Muness to Uyea instead of their walking into Uyeasound and having the Major come across for them. We had investigated Britain's most northerly castle, at Muness, in the morning, and in the course of the afternoon we visited the remarkable early chapel on Uyea. As the years passed and misfortune after misfortune befell the Major's family I often recalled those happy hours with them in Uyea. I saw Sir Basil (as he became) from time to time in Edinburgh, London and Lerwick, but I never happened to visit him in his Shetland home again until shortly before his death, when he was alone in Busta House, a most gallant and stout-hearted old man, struggling against infirmity but determined that his standards should not slip in any particular.

Randal and I were next due, according to our plans, to head for North Yell, and we set out for there in the evening direct from Uyea; I suppose the Major took the ladies back to Uyeasound. Randal and I crossed to Burraness, at the mouth of Basta Voe, where we camped beside the broch — the first night I spent under canvas in Shetland. We at once discovered one of the snags — the lack of clean water on that low-lying peninsula, with plenty of shallow pools but not even a peaty Yell burn. Next day was another truly memorable one. We took the boat round into Basta Voe and up to Colvister, where we drew her up on the beach. Incidentally, it is a commentary on the standards then prevailing in Shetland that wherever we went on our travels we had no hesitation about leaving boat, outboard motor and all our camping gear unattended for the greater part of a day, in complete confidence that we would find everything untouched on our return. We walked up the road to Dalsetter (then still inhabited) and took to the hill for the three miles to the head of Gloup Voe and then along the very steep slope of the Wester Lee of Gloup until we came to Westafirth (then also inhabited). We were welcomed at the house (which, as its normal communication was by boat across Gloup Voe, cannot have had many chance visitors) and the crofter exclaimed that it was a great day: 'The hikers have come to Westafirth'. From Westafirth we followed the wild shores of the uninhabited north-west quarter of Yell round to Lumbister. This was a place in which I had special interest, for Laurence Williamson had told me that my ancestors lived there, and indeed there is documentary evidence of Donaldsons in Lumbister about 1700. I had been there once before, when I walked across the hill from Mid Yell, and it was splendid to see again

that singularly beautiful spot, where the burn issues
through the deep gorge of the Daal into a gio almost
opposite the Point of the Stuis at the mouth of
Whaalfjord. From Lumbister we returned to the boat at
Colvister over two miles or so of hill, past the lochs of
Lumbister and Colvister. I had heard then — and have
had it confirmed since — that this was historic ground, to
the extent that when people lived in Lumbister (where the
walls of four well-built houses still stand) they kept their
boats at the Daal in summer but for the winter took them
across to Basta Voe, using the two lochs on the way.
Many years later I went over the ground again and took a
series of slides which I have used to illustrate this example
of a place where it was customary to make a portage of
boats.

Colvister, at the eastern end of this portage, is said to
be historic too, for tradition has it that in 1567 the Earl of
Bothwell — Queen Mary's Bothwell — spent a night
there when he was in flight from Kirkcaldy of Grange,
who wanted to do justice on him for his part in the
murder of Darnley. As Bothwell happened to be ashore
when Kirkcaldy came in the south mouth of Bressay
Sound and Bothwell's ship had to make a hasty escape by
the north mouth, the Earl was not on board his ship when
it lured Kirkcaldy's vessel, the *Unicorn,* to disaster on the
rock which still bears its name. Bothwell's vessel proceeded to Unst, leaving Bothwell to go on north indepen-
dently. While it is impossible to prove the tradition that
on the way he slept at Colvister, there is no chronological
difficulty, and perhaps the Earl may be regarded as a
pioneer of the 'overland route' to the North Isles. In Unst
Bothwell rejoined his ship and took to the sea, where he
seems to have committed acts of piracy. Then, landing at
Bergen, he was unlucky enough to fall into the hands of
the kinsmen of a girl he had earlier seduced, and, after
some bluster about being the Consort of the Queen of
Scots, was locked up and ended his days at Dragsholm in

Denmark. In the adjoining Faarevejle Kirke I saw his alleged corpse, which — somewhat indecently — used to be on view to the public at the equivalent of 6d. a time, until the present Danish Queen very properly decided to end the exhibition.

From Colvister back to Colvister that day Randal and I must have walked about fifteen miles of Yell 'hill' and 'banks'. There was nothing exceptional about that, for I several times did 25 or more, and we rested our legs when we returned to the boat and set off in the evening for the sixteen-mile run back to Hamnavoe — my longest non-stop run to date.

It had always been our intention to complement our trip eastward to Fetlar and Unst with one westward to the Mainland, and after a few days we set out once again. We had such good conditions that Yell Sound presented no problem, for we were able simply to make across by the north end of Samphrey and pick up the Mainland shore north of Tofts Voe, now the site of the Ferry terminal. Samphrey was another island which always fascinated me and on which I was to land in the following year. It is situated in a commanding position at the southern entrance to Yell Sound, almost precisely equidistant from Yell and the Mainland and by a curious chance its name, on the seventeenth-century Blaeu map, appears as Sancterre, which is close enough to the French for the Holy Land. Now long uninhabited, it had 36 people on it in 1841. We continued to the north-west, to round Mioness and Little Roe (with its red cliffs) and then turn southwards into Sullom Voe. That seven-mile long voe, with its mainly low-lying and barren shores, was a dull and desolate stretch of water in those days, with hardly a sign of activity. I remember eating sandwiches as we plugged rather tediously up the broad inlet. At the head, or nearly the head, of the voe, we went ashore and walked the two miles across a low-lying isthmus (another traditional portage for boats) to the post office at Brae, to send a telegram to reassure the folk in Hamnavoe, who we knew would be wondering how we had fared when we ventured on 'these waster soonds' for which everyone had, very properly, considerable respect. Shetland women of course inherited memories of disasters at sea, and how clearly they were recalled was brought home to me when my Aunt Martha once remarked that the Gloup Disaster of 1881, when 58 men were lost, was, after fifty years, as 'veeve' (vivid) in her mind as on the day she first heard of it. It was almost a convention for the womenfolk to get into a flap and make such an exaggerated exclamation as 'We'll never see him more' when a man went off in a boat, but I am eternally grateful to my mother, who always said, 'I'll never worry about Gordon when he is in a boat'. I do not think I was ever foolhardy, and I did not despise advice. On my first visit with my own boat to Fetlar, I had some thought of returning by the east and south of the island, but I was told, coolly and soberly, 'I don't think you should take your boat round the Snap' and I complied with this sage counsel. (The toughest tussle I ever had with a tide-stream was not in any Shetland sound but in what Hammond Innes called 'the race' that runs between the south end of Lismore and the lighthouse on Eilean Musdile.)

The next stage after our passage up Sullom Voe was the Mavis Grind. At that time I had never been there, and had assessed the likelihood of being able to take a boat across from one of J. D. Rattar's postcards, which suggested that there would be no serious difficulty unless a fence provided an obstacle. As it turned out, there was no problem. The boat, with all moveable gear taken out, could be handled easily up the beach from the North Sea, over the road, through a gate and down the beach to the Atlantic side. It would be more difficult now, for the level of the road has been raised appreciably at this point.

From an inspection of map and chart I had been concerned not only with the crossing of the isthmus but about how we would fare on the other side, where there is a kind of pool with only a very narrow outlet to the western ocean. The exit from the pool (marked Minn on the map) proved to have ample water for our passage, but I had thought there might be trouble beyond, and indeed there was. There had been a spell of westerly wind, it was still a breeze from the west that day, and the waves were piling up as they were funnelled into a channel narrowing towards the Minn. Once we emerged from the pool we were right into the worst of the sea. I had had some idea of venturing out to test conditions, but we really had no option except to proceed, for it would have been hazardous to try to turn the boat. We therefore headed into the sea until we were clear of Turvalds Head and then, as the channel was wider and the sea less packed, it was possible to turn to port and head for Roe Sound, between Muckle Roe and the Mainland.

Even in 1935 Roe Sound was bridged at its narrowest and shallowest point, but I had calculated (correctly as it turned out) that we would be able to get the boat through, though we took to the oars as it was low water and there was a lot of weed in the shallows. Starting up the motor again we resumed our southward progress, but it was by this time well on in the evening and we had to think of a camping site. For purely sentimental or romantic reasons I had thought of Papa Little, where the name suggested an ancient ecclesiastical settlement, and we did land on that rather featureless island, but struck the old snag of lack of good water, so we crossed the narrow sound to Houbansetter on the Mainland. We civilly craved from the crofter permission to pitch our tent on his ground for the night, but he, even more civilly, insisted on taking us in and giving us a bed. Next day we went on the four miles or so up the voe to Aith, where we left the boat and were provided with accommodation for the motor in premises adjoining the shop.

The next stage was one that had been provisionally

G

arranged in advance. My family was friendly with the
Rev H. Pritchard Williams and his wife, Mary Ann
Garriock, and it was understood that should we reach the
west side we would be welcome at the Sandsting Manse.
So from Aith we walked across to the manse on the east
side of Seli Voe and had two nights there, from Friday to
Sunday. On the Saturday our hosts drove us into Lerwick
(where, unknown to us, we were seen by someone who
went up to Burravoe on the steamer next day and took
home news of our progress). On the Sunday evening we
were driven back to Aith, picked up the boat and
uneventfully retraced our steps through Roe Sound,
across the Mavis Grind and into Sullom Voe. There we
succeeded in camping, on the shore below Lunnister. We
spent two nights there and used the intervening day
(Monday) to walk to Hillswick and back. On Tuesday
(13th August) we set out north from Lunnister. Our
objective was now North Roe, where we were more or less
expected, but I was not prepared to forego the chance of
further exploring Northmavine, so we broke our journey
at Collafirth, where we left the boat for a couple of hours
and climbed Roeness Hill. Randal was apt to despise
anything under 3000 feet, but I had to offer him
Shetland's highest hill, of only 1500. This left us ample
time to continue later in the day to North Roe, where we
again got a bed for the night. Next day we walked north
to Fethaland in the morning and in the afternoon re-
crossed Yell Sound, to Westsandwick, in a long and
impressive swell which quite blotted out the land when we
were in the troughs — something we had seen before on
the other side of the Mavis Grind. At Westsandwick we
had hospitality for a night from my good friends at
Scattlands. Next morning (Thursday, 15th August)
Randal and I had a walk north along the Graveland
banks and in the evening returned to Hamnavoe. It had
not been a bad performance — Hillswick, Roeness Hill,
Fethaland and Graveland on four successive days. And

there was an element of a triumphal conclusion with a memorable run from Westsandwick to Hamnavoe, for we had the advantage of a tearing flood tide, running forcefully to the south, and there was no mistaking how as we got down the West Yell coast the current swept us along faster and faster. I had reckoned on taking about an hour and three quarters for the 10½ miles, but we did it in an hour and twenty minutes and must have been doing nine knots at our maximum.

In 1936 I covered some of the same ground again, though with a different confederate to whom it was all new. There was a fortnight or so of what had become more or less routine outings — Burravoe, the Horse, Copister, the Eela and the Mackerel — and a trip to Mid Yell and back. I always look back with a vivid memory and peculiar satisfaction to those long runs to and from Mid Yell, and for some reason it is the southward run that lingers in my mind. There seems to have been a special thrill of satisfaction about clearing Mid Yell Voe, rounding the White Hill of Vatster and settling down to six miles in a straight line to the Windy Clett, passing all the familiar headlands of East Yell, and, if there was a swell, sensing the backwash from each of them as it came up. After these preliminaries we set out on our more extended voyaging, this time starting by going westward. Our objective was North Roe, for besides my confederate I had a 'passenger' in Johnnie Williamson, my Hamna- voe host, who was going on a visit to his former home. We intended to do more or less as we had done the previous year and cross the southern part of Yell Sound, but this time conditions were very different and after two or three minutes which must have been far the most perilous of my whole seafaring career we withdrew from the turbulent waters and hugged the Yell shore to Westsandwick. When we came into the voe there we unexpectedly found the *Earl* at anchor. She had come across from North Roe that afternoon although she was not due to make her call at Westsandwick until the following morning, and she had on board a hapless lady passenger who was faced with the prospect of spending the night on board within a stone's throw of her destination. Tommy Gifford, the mate, hailed us as we came up and asked us to oblige by putting the lady ashore, which we did. In the evening, once the tide had turned, we made the crossing from Westsandwick to North Roe in tranquillity.

My friend and I had four nights in North Roe on that occasion and our most notable expedition (by land) was along the cliffs west of Sand Voe as far as the isle of Uyea, with its famous sand and that rarity in Shetland, a cave on which the sand had so encroached that it could be entered on foot. We returned uneventfully to Hamnavoe. There we spent only two nights before setting out again, this time to the east, for a repeat of the trip to Strand in Fetlar. Again I had a 'passenger' in Bertie Williamson, who took the opportunity to have a few days in Fetlar, where he had a married sister. This time we went ashore briefly at Urie on the way, to break the long haul of just over 20 miles. The day after we arrived in Fetlar the Uyeasound regatta was on, so we took our host's son, 'Bazie', over there for the day. Two days later there was a shorter but more unusual outing. My host Daniel Williamson, the tenant of Strand, kept a few sheep (four, I think) on the Outer Brough of Strand, a grass-covered stack separated from the land by a narrow fissure. He was due to make a call, and as my boat was handier for launching than his, we used her for the trip. We took sheep with us, and it was an exciting business landing on the steep wall of the stack and manhandling animals ashore and up the slope. This Brough, it has always been known, has ancient remains on it of an indeterminate character, too much overgrown with coarse grass when I was there to reveal their nature. I subsequently ascertained, from Bazie, that the passage between the

Brough and Fetlar is very shallow at one point, and this suggests that not so long ago the Brough was not an island but a peninsula linked up by a narrow isthmus.

On our return voyage from Strand to Yell we had some trouble with the engine — a unique experience — which I attributed to the fact that I had procured unsuitable oil in Fetlar, and we had to go ashore at Gossabrough, leave the boat there and 'traivel' over the hill to Hamnavoe. Some days elapsed before it was suitable to 'traivel' back to Gossabrough (carrying a gallon of petrol and some oil), but when we did so there was no trouble about completing our interrupted voyage. The remaining fortnight of the season saw a series of short trips — Copister, Burravoe (four times), Samphrey and Orfasay.

The remaining three seasons of my £30 outfit had nothing to equal the excitement of '34, '35 and '36. In 1937 there was a spell of continuously bad weather and I had no confederate, in 1938 (when I ceased to be a student) I had only a fortnight in Shetland and in 1939 only three weeks. I never again voyaged in my own boat to Fetlar, Unst, the Mainland or even Mid Yell, though I was several times as far as Gossabrough. Thanks to the accidental landing there in 1936 I had made the acquaintance of my cousins, the Hughsons, and their neighbours the Scollays, two families with whom I was welcome year after year thereafter.

Over the seven seasons 1933-39 my mileage added up to nearly 900, about two-thirds with the outboard and a third with oars. The cost added up in the end, according to the precise notes I kept of expenditure of every kind (including petrol at 1/10½ a gallon in Yell and 2/- a gallon in Fetlar) to £42.17.3, but I disposed of the boat and motor for £14.10. The total outlay (with an un-explained discrepancy of 2/2) I noted as £28.5.1. The pleasure added up to something on which no figure or price can be put.

As I implied in chapter 1, I sold the boat, on 18th August 1939, not because I knew that World War II was going to begin a fortnight later but because I knew that my long holidays in Shetland had come to an end for the foreseeable future. The purchaser was A. I. Tulloch, well-known then as a business man and better known in later times for the leading part he has played in the affairs of the islands. I lost track of the craft after I sold her, though I did hear that Mr Tulloch had soon parted with her, and someone told me that he had seen her somewhere on the west side in a neglected condition. I certainly never expected to hear of her, far less see her, again. But there was a sequel which is eloquent of the interest Shetlanders have in a boat and in what might be called the pedigree of a boat. I think about 1960, when I met one of my old Hamnavoe friends, Robbie Petrie, who always had a special interest in boats, he was able to tell me, 'Gordon, your boat is back in Yell. She's at Camb'. A few days later I happened to be on the north side of Mid Yell Voe and went down to the shore at Camb. I spoke to a man I saw there and explained rather diffidently that he would think that I was daft but I was looking for a boat which I had once owned and which now, I was told, was at Camb. 'Oh', he replied, 'then you're Gordon Donaldson'. It was quite evident that as the boat had passed through successive hands over the years her history had been passed on with her. Finally, only two years ago I met the man who then owned her and learned that, curiously enough, she was back, after nearly fifty years, almost exactly where she had been built.

5 ≣ The Rhythm of the Croft

In the 1920s and 1930s crofting was central in the way of life of nearly all Shetlanders outside Lerwick. Almost everyone in the country districts had a croft. The main exceptions were some 'merchants' or shopkeepers, the doctors and the teachers, and some cottars who had only a house and a 'yard' or piece of garden ground. Most ministers by that time no longer worked their glebes, though there was one who did and, so it was said, gave priority to the work on the land: he told the people of a nearby parish, for which he was responsible during a vacancy, that they would have to postpone 'the Sacrament' until the lambing was over. The components of a croft were, first, a yard adjacent to the house, where kale was grown and the hay and corn were stacked for the winter, second, rigs of arable land on which crops of oats, hay and potatoes were grown, and, third, usually a piece of meadow for hay and a piece of inferior land which was not cultivated but used for grazing. These all lay within the dyke which surrounded the township. Outwith the dyke the crofter had rights of grazing and peat-cutting on the scattald, which was land common to the tenants of a township or perhaps of more than one township, and on that common land he could also construct the 'crubs', the square or round enclosures of stone or turf, covered with net, where the seeds were planted for kale, and he could have a henhouse to which the domestic fowls were moved in summer to keep them off the growing crops.

The layout of a crofting area — which meant in

effect the entire Shetland rural landscape — ran very
much to a pattern. Usually each house stood on its own
croft, but as the crofts were usually long and narrow this
did not make one house very distant from its neighbours.
It was not rare, however, for two, three or even four
houses to be built end to end to each other or to form a
compact group huddled together almost in contiguity. I
have reason to believe that where such groups of houses
existed the arable land had until lately been held in run-
rig or rig-rendal, that is, with one tenant's rigs
intermingled with those of others, and that the isolated
houses represent an earlier apportionment into separate
consolidated holdings, but this subject needs investigation. There was often little enough obvious logic about it
all, possibly because the sites for houses might be chosen
either because they were on ground of poor quality or
because of proximity to a well, rather than out of any
notions of symmetry in relation to the whole of the croft. I
knew one case where the houses of two adjacent crofts
were attached gable to gable and the combined structure
straddled the boundary between the two crofts, lying
about two-thirds on one croft and about one-third on the
other, but the tenant of the more southerly croft lived in
the more northerly of the two houses and vice versa, and
each tenant built his peatstack on his neighbour's ground.
I have often wondered, too, why the houses were so often
situated at or near the highest point of the croft, with their
rigs running downhill towards the never distant sea, for
this meant that when the crops were harvested they had to
be carried — usually on the backs of men and women,
especially the latter — up a slope which was sometimes
steep; though admitedly it also meant that in 'voar' or
seed-time the 'muck' from the midden was carried
downhill.

    If life focussed on the croft, the croft focussed mainly
on the cow, cared for as a major asset, for its loss would
have been a disaster. Sheep, after all, in general looked

29 Carting peats 1930

30   The Grey Stane Hole 1922

31   Watering the kye

32   Coming from the well

33   A 'burden' of hay

34   On the North Road, Lerwick, 1922

35 In Hamnavoe 1934

36 On the Mavis Grind 1935

37   Martha and William Donaldson 1922

38   Spinning and knitting 1922

39   Bringing home the peats

40   Team of mowers

41 Caaing the sheep

42 Pony and 'trap' 1931

after themselves, except in the lambing season and on the occasions when they were 'caaed' or gathered for dipping, marking and castrating lambs, 'rooing' or plucking (which took the place of shearing) and taking in lambs for the winter. But the cow needed almost constant attention, expecially in summer. True, some townships turned them out on the scattald, but in general the cow — by this time there was often only one, very rarely more than two — was tethered to a wooden or iron stake on patches of land inside the dykes, patches which were either too poor for cultivation or were lying fallow, and once the hay crop was in they were tethered on the rigs where the grass had been grown. This all meant almost perpetual 'flitting' by moving the stake from one patch of ground to another: 'I see Molly is standing, no' eating; I'll hae tae flit her'. The cow was milked three times a day, so a visit to her in the early afternoon was required. She was brought in for the night to the byre with its low and narrow doorway, through which she had literally to force her way if she had eaten well through the day or if she was in calf. The cow was central in another sense, for most of the crops grown on the croft were after all for her consumption during the winter. When people began to weary of crofting they were apt to complain that all their labour was just to 'feed the coo'.

The group of holdings which composed a township was enclosed by a dyke, so that animals using the common grazing could be excluded from the arable during the growing season. Where a road ran through a township there had to be 'grinds' or gates at the points where it entered and left it. Sometimes only a few yards separated the gate at the extremity of one township from the gate at the near end of the next. One did not journey far without having to stop a vehicle while someone got out to open the gate and then close it again. It was not unknown — though quite unpardonable — for a motor cyclist to apply sufficient force with his machine to a gate to make it open and then go on leaving it open, and there was occasional carelessness. But to leave a gate open even for a few minutes might be disastrous, for there seemed from time to time to be groups of ponies standing nearby just as if they were waiting for such a chance, and they could do enormous damage if they got into the growing crops. In earlier days, before motor vehicles, children in a house not far from a road-gate, when they saw a gig approaching along the road, would run down to the gate to open it and gladly receive a copper thrown to them in reward. Those who have grown up in the era since the cattle-grid superseded the road-gate have no idea what a revolution this was.

I saw little of the 'voar' or seed-time. My rare spring visits never seemed to coincide with the 'delling' that was carried out by a team equipped with Shetland spades, though curiously enough I do recall seeing my Aunt Martha laboriously dragging a harrow over the ground, and I have seen a hand-harrow occasionally in recent years. Nor did I see the cutting or 'casting' of peats in my earlier days, but I have seen that operation many times when I have paid visits in May in recent years, and this is one process which has not been mechanised or changed in any way. I never cease to marvel at the surgical precision with which hundreds of peats are cut, rapidly and cease-lessly, to the same size and shape and laid layer by layer, with interstices to let the air circulate, in a 'dyke' along the top of the bank, all in perfect regularity. For many years I cut some peats on my own peat-moss in Benderloch, using Shetland implements and technique, but never achieved anything like the neatness of the practised hands.

But if I saw little in early days of peat-cutting or even of the 'raising' of them by setting them up in groups of four or five as they gradually dried out, I always had a hand in getting the peats home once they were fully cured. This process has changed a lot. With the popularity of motor vehicles, the tendency has been to use peat-banks as near as possible to the roads, and along the roadside one now finds the parked cars of people working at their peats and not so often heaps of peats waiting to be thrown by ones or twos into a cart but peats already in plastic bags so as to save the time of the lorry which will come to convey them home (and which has to be paid for). But in earlier days, when transport was by wheelbarrows, in kishies on human backs or at best in small carts drawn by Shetland ponies, the peat-banks were as often as not far into the hill. A rough track, to enable carts to get as near the banks as possible, was often made by clearing off the topsoil and reaching a harder surface. But, partly because there was sometimes soft ground or a burn which made even a rough track impracticable, and partly because one individual's peat-banks might be scattered here and there, there was a lot of labour in getting the peats to a point where they could be loaded into a cart. This was where the kishies and the wheelbarrows came in, unless ponies were available which could be loaded up with peats in meshies or open-meshed nets, one on each side of the animal and fastened to the saddle-like 'klibbers' on the pony's back. It could all be a laborious business, some-times needlessly so. I recall that for years we used to barrow peats from some banks down the slope to a burnside, unload them there, pile them into kishies to carry them across the burn and then heap them into a lump at the end of a track which a cart could use. Then someone suggested laying a long plank across the burn, so that the peats could remain in the barrow to be wheeled across; and a large proportion of the accustomed labour was at once eliminated. Occasionally an ingenious individual rigged up a wire stretched between two posts and running down a hillside, on which kishies could be slid down. The final stage, after the cart brought the peats to the house, was to build the peatstack, and here again the characteristic skill, care and neatness came into play to create a fine piece of handiwork. The residue of broken-down or crumbled material left behind when the peats were finally removed from the hill constituted the 'muild' which was used as bedding for the cattle in the byres and in due course helped to constitute the 'muck' for the next year. It was gathered together in heaps called 'roogs' or 'muildy roogs' and covered with turves to keep it dry until it was carried home. It was a good exercise for a stranger to ask him if he knew the meaning of the phrase which sounded like 'We hae a rogue tae feel i' the hill', which was actually a reference to a 'roog' which was to be covered with 'fiels' or turves.

When exactly the peats could be brought home depended largely on the weather, first for curing them and then for the condition of the cart-track, and the work with them consequently often overlapped with the hay-making season, mostly in August. The hay was all cut with the scythe, for I do not remember seeing a small mowing machine until shortly after the War, and it was criticised for not cutting the grass as close to the ground as the scythe would do. I was taught to mow by my great-uncle, who bought a new scythe when he was eighty-seven, and I acquired from the old man a singularly deliberate tempo both in mowing and in sharpening the scythe: indeed I never take up a sharpening-stone without recalling him. But of course neither a man of his years nor an apprentice like me could cut all the grass even on a small croft, and a neighbour was hired for the day, in return for a payment of five shillings, with his meals — the standard day's wage in the thirties. It was always a pleasure to watch a strong, practised mower at work, and some of my memories of specific individuals are of their rhythmic sweep as they laid the grass in swathes and from time to time paused to sharpen the scythe with an equally definite rhythm. Usually one able-bodied and practised mower could easily cope with the few rigs of grass and even a 'meadow' on a small croft, but when a croft had ceased to be cultivated by its absentee tenant and its entire area had been laid down to grass so that all of its three or four acres were producing a hay crop, as many as four mowers might work together, forming up *en échelon* — an impressive sight.

Hay making was sometimes a leading occupation for weeks if the weather was broken. After being cut and laid in swathes it was scattered or 'shakken oot' to give it a chance to dry, then turned over to let sun and air reach the parts which had been in contact with the damp soil. It was then put up in small heaps or 'coles' — often in haste if a shower threatened — and if the coles got well soaked they had to be 'shakken oot' again for another spell of wind and sun. It sometimes seemed that the process would never end. When — or if — the hay was at length cured and the time had come to bring it up to the yard beside the house, it was all carried up the rigs on human backs. I recall only once seeing it being loaded into meshies slung on the flanks of a pony. Usually a doubled rope was laid on the ground, a cole or part of one laid on the ropes, the ropes crossed over and a colleague summoned — 'Come an' knep wi' me' — to tighten the ropes and lift the 'burden' on to one's back. Once in the yard, the next process was 'biggin' da dess', or building the hay into an oblong loaf-shaped stack. All hands were required when this process commenced, and again skill was required if the hay was to be distributed evenly as it was carried into the yard and laid on, stage by stage, being trampled down the while to consolidate it. Finally it was raked down to encourage rain to run off it, a net and ropes weighted with stones laid across it — the cow's winter feeding all secured at last. I sometimes wondered if the cow, eyeing the dess, reflected on what was in store for her.

After the hay, the corn, in September. There was sometimes argument as to which was 'the hairst moon', which was thought essential to 'the hairst' or harvest, for it was well known that 'it's the mune that maets the corn' or puts substance into it. September could become rather stormy, with winds and showers which did the un-harvested oats no good, and although the scythe was regularly used if the crop was standing up well, recourse was often had to 'shearing' with the 'heuk' or 'sickle'. Like, I suppose, most novices with the 'heuk', I took a slice off one of my fingers one blustery September afternoon in 1934, leaving a scar still faintly visible after nearly fifty years.

The new potatoes had been in use for weeks by this time. When a raid was first made on them, my hostess would say, 'I'll hae tae purl for some' and she would grope in the earth under the shaws, selecting tubers fit for boiling and leaving the rest to mature further. It was a great addition to the menu when the new potatoes became readily available, for Shetland 'taaties' have a flavour all of their own. With Shetland lamb they were a treat, and the highest tribute one can pay to them is that, especially if accompanied by plenty of Shetland butter, they made even dried piltocks palatable. The lifting or 'henting' of the main crop usually took place in October, after I had left.

Each crofter had his rights in the scattald or common grazing outside the hill dykes, for apportionment was hardly if at all known in my experience until after World War II. The sheep of all the tenants ran together, but each tenant's animals were identified, as they had been for centuries, by markings on their ears. Any operation connected with sheep — dipping, castrating lambs, 'rooing' or plucking off the old wool as the new growth pushed it out, taking in lambs for slaughter, for sale or for wintering — was a communal effort in which every tenant and his dog took part. On the appointed day, provided the weather was suitable, there was a general muster. There were understood stances for every individual — and his dog — and those who had the longest distance to 'traivel' set out first, for a plod of perhaps three miles or more to the point, often on a watershed, where he had to begin driving the sheep. It was a great sight to see the sheep beginning to move in response to the dogs, and gradually concentrate into a flock which was driven, with much barking on the part of dogs which had sometimes more zeal than finesse, towards the crö or enclosure where there was usually a dipper. If the operation was dipping, a record had to be kept of each man's animals, so that he could be charged his share of the cost of the dip and of any maintenance to the dipper, and this involved a 'clerk to the crö', who sat by the dipper with a notebook and made a record in the traditional tally form ⧼⧽ /// and so on as the men engaged in the dipping, recognising the marks, sang out, 'Gilbert Cogle a lamb' or 'John Williamson a yow'. The dipping was done quite simply by seizing the animal, turning it upside down and holding it by the legs while it was immersed in the dipper, which was constructed with a sloping end so that the creature could scramble up into the 'dreeper' and then be 'slippit' to join other dipped members of the flock. The crö had to be reasonably near a burn to obtain the water in which the dipping fluid was mixed. One of the purposes of a 'caa' was to cull an occasional lamb for butchering, and late in the season the lambs generally were separated from their mothers and taken 'home' for wintering. Cottars, although they had little or no arable land, sometimes did have a few sheep, and one female cottar, not of very strong intellect, proposed to imitate her neighbours and take a lamb home, but was reminded that she had nothing to feed it on, and retorted, 'There's plenty o' girse at the ben windae'. Sheep were apt to cast a lot of their 'oo' or wool before rooing took place, and strands of it were pulled from their sides when it caught in heather. In thrifty times, it was worth while for children to collect such 'hentilags' and so add to the family income.

Very often a single crofter had sheep in more than

one 'caa', so he might be involved for two or three days
when there was anything to be done to the sheep. Sheep,
by the way, generally stayed in very much the same area
of hill and each of them — most of them known individually by their owners — would turn up without fail
in the same 'caa'. Within their chosen area they moved
quite a lot, cropping as they went, and it was well known
that they moved up and down with the tides, presumably
because they sometimes cropped the seaweed in 'the ebb'.

The purpose of the hill dyke and its related grinds or
gates was of course to separate the scattald from the arable
land and keep the grazing animals off the growing crops in
the summer months. Once the crops had all been gathered
in, 'the ockrigart was slippit', that is, grinds were opened
or removed and the animals had freedom to range over the
rigs which had been forbidden to them for several months
and graze on what had been left after the hay and corn had
been harvested. They were still excluded from the yards
adjacent to the houses, where the hay dess and the screws
of corn were concentrated. When spring came again, the
grinds were closed and the animals once more restricted to
the scattald. Between the wars the dykes were still made of
dry stone or more frequently of turf (often on a stone
foundation), topped with stakes and ropes, though even
then post and wire fencing was beginning to supersede the
more traditional structures, which needed frequent
attention and were not always effective against some of the
extraordinarily lively and enterprising sheep (occasionally
restrained by having a triangle of sticks fastened round
their necks, in the hope of preventing them from getting
through the stakes and ropes or even a wire fence).

Already between the wars a few crofts were no longer
worked, partly because the security of tenure granted to
crofters in 1886 had produced absentee tenants who have
been as mischievous as absentee landlords ever were. But
until World War II most of the crofts which were
occupied were still being worked. For a time thereafter it

seemed that crofting might take a new lease of life, for many tenants applied for and received apportionments of the common grazing and carried out reclamation — deep-ploughing, surface-treatment and re-seeding — with in some cases spectacular results, at least for a time. Mechanisation at last came along to lighten the labour, for small tractors became available, and the processes which used to occupy so many hands — turning over the ground in 'voar', mowing or reaping, 'shakkin' oot' the hay, gathering the hay or corn and conveying it to the yard — were all now done with mechanical help. But ultimately a dwindling and ageing population made crofting less viable, and an economy based increasingly on money made it a less attractive proposition to devote time and effort to activities which were a persistent tie and brought in little cash. Then any prospects that a revitalised agriculture might play a dominant part in the Shetland rural economy vanished with the oil developments and the inflated wages they offered. While middle-aged men were still disposed to carry on crofting, partly because they liked the rather easy-going life and being their own masters, younger men were not attracted to work on the land. Far more land has gone out of cultivation since the crofters gained security than ever went out of cultivation as a result of the 'clearances' by landlords of which modern agitators try to make capital. The cow, that creature which once dominated rural life, has become almost a rarity. There were over 20,000 cattle in 1870, only 7000 in 1970. In 1980 I was told that in Mid Yell and North-a-voe, where a generation previously most households had been working their crofts, there was now not a single cow, and this is not exceptional.

For the older generation, who had known no other way of life, the end of working the croft was a terrible wrench. I recall a letter in which my hostess of many years told me that her husband had decided to do no more voar work. This, she said, meant that 'the cow will go in

H

the autumn, and' she added with poignant understate-
ment, 'I'll be sorry'.

In my early days in Shetland I used to say that one of
the blessings of the place was the freedom of movement,
even within the enclosed land of a township, because of
the absence of fences, especially fences with barbed wire.
But one of the changes in the landscape which has
followed from turning over crofts to grazing has been the
proliferation of post-and-wire fences to enclose areas
abandoned for cultivation and now simply cropped by
sheep. When this caper first began, in the 1920s, there
was a measure of resentment at the obstacles thus placed
on what may not have been rights of way but were at any
rate traditional paths. I remember my father, who was
the most mild-tempered of men, remarking sharply that
'this woman has fenced in this ground' and so obstructed
the 'sooth gait' which had been the customary route out
of Lower Hamnavoe. The fence did not indeed prevent
determined walkers from adhering to the old route, but it
destroyed a tradition. Nowadays — when the situation
has changed again with the provision of tarred roads
through the townships — the old freedom of movement
has vanished.

A croft, it should not be necessary to make clear, is a
piece of land and has had that meaning throughout all the
centuries when the word has been used in Scotland. The
more specific modern meaning is a tenant's individual
holding, comprising arable land in which he has sole
occupancy, with, in addition, rights in a common grazing
which he shares with other tenants. The crofting system
of individual tenancies, as distinct from the earlier pattern
of group tenancies which used to prevail generally
throughout Scotland, developed from the late eighteenth
century. Crofting tenure attained special legal recognition and crofters received valuable privileges, especially
fixed rents, security of tenure and the right of succession
either by inheritance or by bequest, in the Crofters

Holdings Act of 1886 and later legislation. The crofting counties, in all of which such tenures were common, were Shetland, Orkney, Caithness, Sutherland, Ross and Cromarty, Inverness-shire and Argyll. In Shetland the overwhelming majority of the agricultural holdings are crofts; larger farms and owner-occupiers are extremely rare. Yet while 'croft' is the technical term, the word is not in everyday use in Shetland, where an individual's holding is commonly known as his 'toun', a term which has an even longer pedigree in this sense than 'croft' has. I recall once in early days going down to 'flit the coo' and being mildly rebuked because I had put her 'half a tether's length on Robbie Bruce's toun'.

These remarks are necessary because the term croft is often used, quite wrongly, to mean a cottage. How often one sees a town dweller who is seeking a country house for holidays or retirement advertising for 'a croft', when if he were presented with a croft he would not know what to do with it. This silly usage possibly received encouragement from one Rowena Farre, whose *Seal Morning* purported to depict a way of life in an unidentified part of Sutherland, where she lived in a 'croft' which 'consisted of a kitchen-cum-parlour, a small bedroom apiece and a tiny room which was used as a workroom, or a guest room when we had visitors' and where one of her neighbours lived in a 'two-roomed croft'. Possibly the lady lived in a suburban bungalow called 'The Croft' and there committed to paper a description of a never-never-land in which there are Eskimoes in Iceland, Tiree is in the Outer Hebrides, Highlanders speak Lowland Scots, wet peat is loaded straight from the bank into panniers to be carried to the house, a three-hundredweight seal could lie in her lap and could play a mouth organ: whether it held the instrument in its flippers or a human accomplice held the instrument while the creature puffed and blew at appropriate moments is not disclosed. The book has no photographs.

However, while a croft was not a house, a croft had a
house on it, and the house was comprehended in the
tenancy — at least its shell was, for interior constructions
ranked as 'improvements'. And a croft, if it was worked,
presupposed a resident crofter. The unimproved house
was a single-storey structure of two apartments, the 'but'
or kitchen-livingroom and the 'ben', furnished as a kind
of sitting-bedroom but essentially a sleeping apartment.
Doors and windows were small, presumably because
stone was so much more plentiful in Shetland than wood,
but it is hard to see why walls were so low, when there was
plenty of stone to build them higher. The small doorways
and low ceilings seemed singularly inappropriate,
because while Shetland animals are much smaller than
average and can be fitted into tiny outhouses when they
are indoors at all, the human beings are often of more
than average height. I have seen a family who could stand
to their full height only between the joists carrying the
ceiling and who in practice moved around the house with
a perpetual stoop. Windows were not as a rule made to
open, so that ventilation was by the door and the
chimneys. The timbers and planking of the ceilings, if not
whitewashed, were mellowed to a pleasant shade by the
peat reek. If a severe gale was blowing — and it often was
— against the front door of the house, it was considered a
hazard to open the door lest the force of the wind should
lift off the roof. But many houses, even before they were
otherwise improved, had wooden porches which gave
some protection, and if the outhouses were built in front
of the dwellinghouse they provided a kind of wind-break.
I recall seeing 'but' ends with floors of earth or of rough
concrete, but the ben end seemed always to have a
wooden floor. Between the but and the ben was usually a
small apartment called a closet, which could enter either
from the but end or from the space inside the front door,
and which might have a back door. Here water and milk
were kept, the kirn stood, there was a basin for washing.

The closet was apt also to house rubber boots and the bootjack if there was one. On this hinged one of the best practical jokes every played on me. There was at one stage some good-natured chaffing about the hour at which I returned from courting expeditions, and my hostess declared she would devise a means of finding out. One stormy night I set forth wearing rubber boots which were a very good fit and which, it was well known, I could not discard without a bootjack. When I returned — of course to find the household in bed — I made my way through the but end to the door of the closet and when I opened it there was an unearthly clatter of tins and other objects which had been skilfully piled behind it.

As houses developed beyond the strict but and ben, to the extent of having attic accommodation (often very restricted in height and reached by an extremely steep stair), it became rather unusual to see a bed in the but end — contrary to the quite usual practice in the south, where the kitchen normally had a bed. There might be in the but end a box-bed, with a door like a cupboard, but 'ben' and in the attic the beds, though they might be fixtures against linings or partitions, were not boxed. Before the more usual type of mattress came into use, there were mattresses filled with chaff and laid on boards. The ben end, while rarely used for any other purpose than as a sleeping apartment, had certain pretensions to gentility — an upholstered or basket armchair, a table of better quality wood, with a cover on it, a rag-rug in front of the fire-place and some of the abundant sheepskin rugs. If the reader reflects that there were plenty of articles which could harbour fleas, his deduction is justified.

The but end was more austere. The chairs were mostly simple, home-made affairs of white wood, sometimes supplemented by equally plain stools. There was no upholstery, but sometimes cushions. Apart from the table and the dresser, the main piece of furniture was the characteristic 'resting-chair', commonly called 'da share' and best described as a wooden settle, which, though sometimes bearing signs of unprofessional work, could be so well-proportioned as to be handsome. It seems to have been almost obligatory to place it on the wall which had the window and which ran at right-angles to the wall with the hearth. 'Da share' could be cushioned or padded, and of course it could serve as an auxiliary addition to the sleeping accommodation. The dog's place was under 'da share', and a humane owner might cut out part of a spar to make it less of a feat for the dog to get in and out. A well-trained dog would never offer to stir from its place until called, and there was no question of the dog having the run of the house: 'Open doors, dugs gang ben' was a proverb. The dresser, with cupboards beneath and shelves above, to hold china, cutlery and some foodstuffs, was sometimes a fixture, built in with the wooden lining.

The but end was often festooned with dried fish which, after being salted and exposed at the gable of the house to sun and air, were now taking on their final curing in the peat-reek as they hung on lines or wooden rods above the fireplace. The mantelpiece was usually a repository for decorated tea-caddies and sometimes a pair of those china dogs which were long despised but are now once more prized. On the walls there was sure to hang at least one, sometimes two or three, calendars from the local 'merchants' or shopkeepers, each usually a single large sheet showing the whole year beneath a coloured reproduction of a picture. Shetlanders liked pictures on their walls, especially pictures of ships, and most houses had some examples of paintings of sailing ships or early steamers, not infrequently in impossible seas. The conventional marine artist gave priority to accurate representation of the ship (which could be meticulous in detail) and the setting was a secondary consideration. Besides, there was a favourite in a print of 'The Gospel Ship', a full-rigged sailing vessel with a scriptural text on each sail. Framed biblical texts, sometimes with floral decoration, might add to the display. Incongruously, there could be devotional prints showing The Sacred Heart, Madonna and Child and that kind of thing, which had obviously been brought home from Roman Catholic countries. Other souvenirs of distant voyaging were pieces of 'whalebone', a walrus tusk, a swordfish's saw or a turtle shell, and there was usually a ship in a bottle. At one side of the but window hung a barometer, frequently consulted. (The scores of ship-pictures which were thrown out as junk would now be highly prized. A dealer in Edinburgh told me that when he started in business he was warned that there were two objects he must never buy, namely pictures of cows and pictures of ships, but that things were different now.)

Associated with the house were the other buildings necessary for the work of the croft — barn, byre, lamb-house and hen-house. Sometimes house, barn and byre were in a continuous line, sometimes the outbuildings or some of them were detached, perhaps opposite the house and with their doors facing it. The latter arrangement had advantages in bad weather, but, when the barn adjoined the house, there was even greater convenience in a communicating door, which had been condemned by the sanitary authorities but sometimes persisted. It was a further piece of ingenuity in a harsh climate — and again abhorrent to the hygienists — that some houses had a dip well within the but end. In Houlland and Littlester, South Yell, this was true of several of them.

As I mentioned in the first chapter, there were changes in the houses even between the Wars, but the changes have been even greater in more recent years. The coming of piped water resulted in the construction of extensions to contain at least a bathroom; the work was often done by the talented amateurs so common in Shetland and, while competent, was not always sightly. More recently still, in the affluent oil age, a considerable number of new houses have been built by private individuals. While building labour is scarce and costly, the handy Shetlander is capable of erecting a pre-fabricated house himself, and the results are sometimes very pleasing. The versatility of the Shetlander is something at which I never cease to marvel. In earlier days a jack of all trades by necessity, and capable of handling the scanty and often intractable local materials to erect buildings, fashion furniture and implements and construct superb boats, the modern Shetlander has kept abreast of technical developments and has taken to electrical, radio and automobile engineering and to modern building techniques, with striking success. No one can teach Shetlanders anything about Do it Yourself.

The new houses are often in sharp contrast to the traditional houses, and their conspicuousness is all the greater in a landscape like Shetland's, where very little will grow around a house and gardening is the most dispiriting of activities. The new houses do look somewhat raw against a stark moor or hillside. Yet, apart from some of the larger clumps of council houses, the predominant pattern is still that of the little house, often of course vastly enlarged and improved, sitting on its own croft or what used to be its croft, now often uncultivated. This is a consequence of the advantageous terms that crofters gain from security of tenure. giving them the benefits of proprietorship without its liabilities and responsibilities, and at nominal rents, sometimes it is said fixed in the late 1880s and never raised since. Anyone who can sit in effect rent-free on the site of an existing house has a strong disincentive to abandon it.

It has been characteristic of economic and social changes, in Shetland as elsewhere, that while the homes of crofters and cottars have become indistinguishable in their standards from middle-class homes in the south, the one-time mansions of the lairds have, like large country houses elsewhere, become what it might be suitable to call 'redundant', for their impoverished owners were unable to maintain them. The great houses of the Bruces — Sumburgh and Symbister — have become an hotel and a school, and the historic home of the Giffords — Busta — is now also an hotel. Even houses of more modest size are now too often disused and roofless — the old home of the Neven-Spences in Uyea, Windhouse, Dalsetter, Belmont and many more. It is refreshing to see one or two instances of rehabilitation and restoration — the Aald Haa at Burravoe, the Haa of Gloup and Burrastow. But it should be said that the ambitions of Shetland lairds seem sometimes to have outrun their resources and the result was a degree of useless grandiosity. Windhouse in Yell was fitted with huge gates and gate-posts, but they abutted on a very ordinary Shetland dyke; Brough Lodge in Fetlar (now abandoned and wrecked by vandals) was the most extraordinary Gothic 'folly', with the laundry designed as an imitation chapel; and in Bressay there is a fantastic mausoleum.

The crofting economy was essentially a subsistence economy in the strict sense that it was designed to support life and not to earn money. The croft provided most of the basic foodstuffs: potatoes, milk, butter, eggs, some lamb or mutton; and there was usually fish to be had for the taking: haddock, whiting, mackerel, saithe, and an occasional sea-trout. The foodstuffs that had to be bought were few. First the inevitable sugar and tea. (I do not recall coming across coffee very often until fairly recently, but of course Instant Coffee has transformed the position for that beverage.) Then flour, tinned goods, loaf-bread, cakes and the biscuits to which Shetlanders were so addicted. The 'loaf' obtained from the shop was apt to be regarded as a delicacy in contrast to the home-baked bannocks, commonly called 'bread', but how mistaken this idea was, especially as it was something of a problem in the North Isles to obtain bread that was anything like fresh. A bakery in Mid Yell had a short life, and bread was imported sometimes from Voe, sometimes from

Lerwick, sometimes from Aberdeen and sometimes —
incredibly — from Glasgow; it was hygienically wrapped,
of course, but it was sometimes green by the time it was
bought in a shop in Yell. The diet was potentially sound
and adequate, and palatable, but some thought that
people did not always make full use of what they had at
hand and turned to makeshift bites instead. 'It's biscuits
and tea that's ruining Shetland', declared Mr Carson, the
Fetlar minister. Tea was certainly drunk with amazing
frequency, as an accompaniment to the snacks and meals
which punctuated the working-day. Morning tea in bed;
tea at breakfast; tea at noon (the 'twal' or 'twellus',
presumably meaning 'twelve hours'); tea after dinner,
about 2 p.m.; tea at tea-time; 'eight o'clocks', which
speaks for itself; and possibly tea at a late supper.

When my mother was visiting Yell regularly in the
1930s she introduced some innovations in the diet, partly
by having an occasional parcel sent from Edinburgh. I
recall, for instance, the first appearance of tomatoes on
the table in Lower Hamnavoe. My mother also thought it
would be good to have sausages, which were not then
stocked by shops in Yell. They would not have survived
being sent from Edinburgh, but she arranged with a
Lerwick butcher to send two pounds of sausages up on a
Friday with the steamer. I have no idea what sausages
cost then — probably about a shilling a pound — and the
freight was tenpence, which was denounced as extortion-
ate. Of course in recent years, with the introduction of
electricity, refrigeration has transformed the situation
both in the shops and in the homes.

The money income of the croft — leaving aside
money from other sources like part-time or full-time
employment — came from the sale of the wool-crop, the
sale of lambs (though the average crofter hardly carried a
big enough stock to permit this), the sale of a calf.
Sometimes a few eggs were sold at the local shop — at
sixpence a dozen I seem to remember. At times the export

of lambs, even for those who had fair-sized stocks, was hardly profitable because of the freight charges, and there was the usual story that at the end of the day when all expenses had been paid the seller received a few pence in stamps. Growing indignation at this led in 1932 to the chartering by some Shetland sheepowners of a steamer, the *Great Western,* to carry their lambs at 2/6 a head against the North of Scotland's charge of 3/1 — if I remember the figures aright. It was very successful as far as it went — I remember seeing the vessel coming into Mid Yell — but the North of Scotland soon retorted by cutting their charge to 1/7 or something like that. However, when the crisis was over the North Company did not revert to their original 3/1.

Tiny crofts, often of only three or four acres, had never been intended either to offer full-time employment or provide a livelihood, but had been meant to be supplemented by some other occupation. The older pattern had been for crofting to be combined with employment in commercial fishing, but already by the time I first knew Shetland this had largely vanished. A few men did go to the herring fishing in the season, but in the main commercial fishing had become a full-time occupation and the occasional fishing which crofters did was for their own consumption and not for sale. Supplementary employment and supplementary income had to come from other sources. The most steady income of a crofting family came not directly from the produce of the croft but indirectly, through the wool its sheep produced, from the expert and unwearied fingers of the womenfolk. Amid all the changes, all the ups and downs, in the Shetland economy, knitted goods — the 'hosiery' of Shetland usage — proved remarkably stable as marketable commodities. In recent years the high wages obtainable in oil-related employment were detrimental to the output of hosiery, but it now appears that, as oil-related employment dwindles, the knitting machines are

coming out again. Women sometimes made another contribution to the family income by the money they earned
by seasonal employment as herring gutters, not only in
Lerwick and at other 'stations' in Shetland but at herring
ports in the south, to which they moved as the herring
migrated in the autumn.

A man could pick up a few shillings now and again
by mowing or by carting peats, and in each port at which
the steamer called there were usually four men employed
to man the flitboat, a job which, small though the wages
might be, constituted registered employment and gave
the flitmen the benefit of National Insurance. Some
Shetlanders turned their versatile craftsmanship to
account by occasional jobbing. And, even in the days
when the roads hardly deserved the name, there was
road-work. But the main paid employment for men was
seafaring, which played a central role for generations and
had a great effect not only on the economy but on the
whole outlook of the Shetland community. One
remembers how the local newspapers used to carry
columns of reports on ship movements, so that, in the
absence of other information, the folks at home knew of
the approximate whereabouts of absent kinsmen and
friends. In the lists, asterisks proudly drew attention to
the very large number of vessels which were commanded
by Shetlanders. This service in the merchant navy,
combined with the migration of many Shetlanders to
settle in ports like Leith and Shields and in many places
overseas — often after service in ships trading to faraway
parts — made the outlook remarkably cosmopolitan and
did a lot to counteract the isolation Shetland might
otherwise have felt, especially in the days when facilities
for spreading news were so much more limited than they
have come to be now. It was illuminating to be in a
crofter's home on mail day when a Shetland mother was
opening the letters which had come from her sons:
Andrew had settled in Australia; Johnnie was in

Edinburgh; Willie was on one of the 'City' boats trading to the far east; Henry was master of a steamer trading across the North Sea; and so on.

The traditional pattern was in the main that a man went off sailing for a year or two, then came home for a spell before going away again, so that crofting and sailing were combined. However, the method of recruitment for the merchant navy was revolutionised during and after the Second World War, with the creation of what was popularly known as 'the Pool' and the introduction of preparatory training for boy entrants. It was no longer possible for a boy to go away and expect to begin his seafaring career by joining a ship without any formal training, nor was it any longer possible for a man simply to seek employment casually and leave his employment equally casually. This bureaucracy disrupted a whole way of life, and the new arrangements bore hard on Shetlanders — though it should be said that the mercantile marine must have suffered too by making it more difficult to recruit men who, though without formal training, had learned all there was to know about ships and the sea from first-hand experience and from what they had heard from their elders. The only story I recall hearing about a young Shetlander who went to sea and revealed ignorance of the ways of ships was this. My friend Johnnie was at the wheel with the skipper on the bridge, while another Shetlander, on lookout forrard, shouted something which the skipper could not understand. After a second attempt, the skipper asked Johnnie what the lookout was saying, and Johnnie was able to translate 'Da red lantern is slokkit, sir', as 'The port light has gone out'.

In the nineteenth century an alternative to service in the merchant navy was service in whaling vessels working in the Arctic seas, especially around the Davis Straits. In the twentieth century the antarctic became the area for whaling, and in the 1920s some Shetlanders were in South Georgia. Then, in the years after the Second World

War, there was a brief period when whaling in the south engaged a large number of young Shetlanders.

Families which for one reason or another had none of the sources of money income which were available handled scarcely any cash at all and there was, at least in pecuniary terms, real poverty. The mother of one such family was one Sunday afternoon visiting a neighbour who was, as so many people were on Sunday afternoons, engaged in writing letters to friends, and she remarked, 'I would need to be writing too, but I haven't the money for the stamps'. That lady's grand-daughter, incidentally, earned over £200 a week in domestic service at one of the construction camps in connection with the Sullom Voe oil base. That discloses, in a couple of sentences, the transformation of Shetland.

It must of course be remembered that even crofters who were, by the standards of the time, above the level of poverty, handled little money. Even the acquisition of groceries and other supplies from the local shop did not as a rule involve a cash transaction. Such supplies were usually handed over the counter in exchange for knitted goods. This practice was generally denounced as unfair, and not without reason. Very often the shop had a local monopoly, for there was no transport in those days to make it possible to purchase elsewhere, and it was pointed out that the merchant, as the shopkeeper was rather grandiosely styled, got a profit on the goods and a profit also on the hosiery when he sold it. And there was sometimes very little in it for the knitter. I recall one woman getting an order from the shop for a spencer. It so happened that she did not have the appropriate yarn at hand, and had to buy a supply, which cost her 1/8. When she finished the spencer and took it to the shop she was allowed 1/6. Of course she was left with yarn which she had not used, but even so it did seem hard. Yet she characteristically thought it rather a joke. There was another woman, an outstanding knitter, who took a jumper to the merchant and, admiring it as she handed it over, remarked that she thought it deserved more than the standard price. 'Yea', replied the merchant, 'dat is guid. I'll gie dee extra. Bit I'll tak it aff da groceries'. This too was thought a piece of wit. The fact is that poverty, if poverty is indeed the word for it where there was no poverty of spirit, bred neither resentment nor envy nor greed nor jealousy or any of the other deadly sins which have been fostered by sociologists and politicians. 'We aye hed enough' was the Shetlander's philosophical attitude.

Incidentally, the problem of raising money for church funds in an impecunious society was solved by the members of a Women's Guild in Shetland donating knitted goods which were sent to the Guild of a congregation in the south, where they were sold for money. It was through this machinery (when my mother acted on behalf of the Guild of a church in Edinburgh) that my family was first associated with the occupants of the Sandsting manse.

The dress which was customary in Shetland in the 1920s and 1930s had no relation to the bright colours of the knitted goods which were then being so plentifully produced. Women habitually wore very dark, often black, blouse and skirt, and the hap or shawl, crossed over the chest and round to the back — ideal for cold and stormy days — was almost a uniform, usually also in dark brown or black. Men, like the women, tended to wear dark clothes, but the dungarees which they favoured between the wars as working clothes did not change much when they gave way to jeans. I may say I hardly ever saw rivlins, the traditional shoes of untanned cow's hide. The habitual footwear was rubber boots or wellingtons, varied by canvas-and-rubber shoes; both probably contributed to the rheumatism which was endemic. In recent years, perhaps as one by-product of affluence, Shetlanders seem to have knitted more for themselves and not just as a commercial enterprise, with the result that some extremely attractive, indeed handsome, knitted garments, in bright colours, have become common for men, women and children — a feature which adds charm to the modern Shetland scene.

The life of the crofting community was much affected by population changes. When I first knew Shetland its population had fallen from its maximum of over 31,000 (in 1861) to 25,000; and I saw it decline further, census by census, until it fell to 17,000. After that, thanks to the oil developments, there was a recovery of several thousands, but by that time the figure was no longer relevant to the crofting community. At local level, one could not fail to be conscious of a vast change. In the community which I knew best, there had been within living memory over 60 people, but I saw it fall to less than twenty. There were curious variations from one area to another. In Hamnavoe, South Yell, there are still seven occupied houses (against a maximum of eleven which I knew), while in adjoining Houlland there are only two or three occupied houses (as against nine I knew). However, within families there has been a melancholy repetition of the same pattern of the number of individuals dwindling generation by generation, with men and women either remaining unmarried or marrying and having no children. One example: in one generation six sons and two daughters, only two of whom married and only one of whom had children; in the next generation only one man and one woman, both of them childless; in the third generation, therefore, nil. Equally, I could name two families which each consisted of three daughters and one son, and not one of the eight married. It seemed quite clear that certain families were doomed to extinction.

With an inordinate number of bachelors and spinsters there were some improbable situations. One might see three eligible bachelor-sons in a house next door to one which was the home of three apparently attractive daughters, of similar ages, but not one pair made a match of it. There was a lot of courtship which never led to marriage, indeed there was almost an institution of perpetual courtship. A couple might start 'going together' or 'walking out together' in their teens and continue the ritual for their life-times, almost as a matter of habit, yet never marry. Some men seemed simply never to shake off the habit of visiting a particular house, as a matter of routine, on Wednesdays and Saturdays, although any serious object in the visit had long vanished. It was sometimes said that marriage was inhibited by the lack of houses, where almost the only houses in existence were those on crofts. A son might indeed bring his wife into his parents' home, but this was not necessarily an ideal solution and was often quite impracticable on grounds of space. It should, however, be said that some family units comprised a number of individuals whose relationship to each other was not immediately obvious to a visitor who might be introduced to them all only by their Christian names. A mother, her son and daughters (one married), the son's wife and the son's two children made up a household which it was not easy to take in at a glance. It may be that the real problem about houses arose from the Crofters' Act which gave security of tenure and the right to assign crofts without insisting that they be cultivated or that the houses on them should be maintained; absentee tenants meant unoccupied houses. If the landlord had retained his old rights he would have been able to allot the tenancy of croft and house to a young couple who would have lived in it and worked it. One heard a good many complaints about houses which were standing 'vod' or empty when people would have been prepared to take them. A further complication was that in the Scottish rating system the landlord then had to pay rates on unoccupied houses, so that he was tempted, as soon as a house was vacant, to take off the roof. The whole situation about courtship and marriage, about housing and about some of the causes of

I

depopulation is far more deserving of investigation than many a subject of a sociological thesis.

One got the impression — though it may just have been a reflection of nostalgia for 'the good old days' — that when the population had been larger crofting had been very different. There had been far more cattle, for one thing: there had to be, even though it must have meant keeping the wretched animals at starvation level. But many hands had made light work at every stage of the crofting programme. And there had been more jollification at times like 'hairst' when there were more young people to enjoy fun together.

The general rhythm of the croft was constant because it depended on the seasons, but within the general rhythm there was a lot of variation, dictated by the weather. Whether the weather is among the things that have changed is often debated, but both recorded data and my own impressions indicate that it is not. There were indeed always good years and bad years. One that stands out in my mind is 1931, when I was in Shetland for seven weeks and while there were a few — a very few — days on which rain fell there was not a single occurrence of what could be called a wet day. In 1937, on the other hand, for six weeks there seemed to be almost incessant cloud and mist and a cold wind, so that for a fortnight I never had my boat out. I got a taste in August 1979 of one of the most disastrous seasons in living memory, which was fatal to a lot of hay and peats and seemed likely to be a final sickener for those who were still crofting. Then in May-June 1980 I was fortunate to get the tail end of a remarkably dry spell, at a time when there had been hardly any rain for six or seven weeks. It is not that the weather, even when good, is necessarily settled. But the very changeability of it is an advantage. Usually if it is raining in the morning it will dry up at mid-day or at 3 p.m. or at 6 p.m. In the West Highlands, by contrast, if it is raining in the morning it is liable to rain the whole of that day, the whole of the next and the whole of the day after that.

The fact that there were stable patterns in the weather is suggested by some of the sayings which were current. Those streaky, wispy clouds which precede strong winds were the 'horses' manes and mares' tails' which 'make tall ships carry low sails'. On a blustery day, when the wind comes and goes with the showers, 'If the wind before the rain, hoist your topsails up again; if the rain before the wind, your topsail halliards you must mind'. Certain sayings about the pattern of the weather within a week were current. 'A cambric Monday makes a canvas week and a canvas Monday makes a cambric week' meant that the rest of the week would be different from Monday, and experience — not only in Shetland — seemed to show that a fine Monday morning was a bad sign and a wet Monday morning a good sign. Then 'Wednesday's weather is true' meant that the weather would remain constant throughout the day, which experience in Shetland seemed to bear out. Friday was 'either the best day or the worst day of the week', and I do remember some superbly good and some extremely bad Fridays. 'Saturday's weather is fine' had much truth about it too, for my own usual assignment on a Saturday morning was a visit to Burravoe to get the time at the Post Office and meet the steamer, and I do not recall ever being stopped by the weather. It is barely credible that the pattern of the weather was determined by the week's calendar, and yet there seemed to be something in it. Some made their predictions by the phases of the moon, which, whether or not they affected the weather, profoundly affected the freedom one had to move about after dark — except, of course, in midsummer, when there was daylight all night.

With a fair experience of Shetland in most seasons, I would say that in my opinion it looks at its best in August. There is then a mellowness about the landscape, which is

apt to seem harsh and stark in spring and early summer.
Spring comes late and the land tends to retain a somewhat
bleached appearance until well through May, especially
if, as I have several times experienced, there has been
severe and snowy weather in April. In June and July,
when the harshness disappears, the landscape is too
uniformly green. But in August, in crofting areas — at
least where the land is still cultivated — the grass has been
mown and the yellowing coles of hay stand on the green
rigs, while nearby the corn begins to ripen and contrasts
in its turn with the maturing green of the potato shaws;
and in late August the heather blooms. It was my good
fortune to be in Shetland in August every year from 1929
to 1939 as well as in many later Augusts and perhaps I am
apt to regard that month as a norm. It is on the whole a
good month for weather, too, though from time to time
there are 'Lammas spates' (dated by 'Old Lammas',
about the 12th of the month) and there may well be spells
of heavy, warm fog — but how rewarding it is when the
sun breaks through. The fine August of 1930 was
punctuated by a heavy thunderstorm which had its worst
effects in the north Mainland, where it started off
landslides, and the August of 1935, which had a good
record, was preceded (on 19th-20th July) by floods which
caused landslides and destroyed a number of bridges. I
recall, too, in August 1930, when we were at the 'Eela' on
a very still, quiet evening, a thunderstorm sprang up and
we heard the heavy rain falling on the water as it
approached the boat. We took refuge for a time in the
shepherd's hut on Orfasay. But such occasional brief
thunderstorms are only the inevitable hazard of warm,
calm weather. It is always worth while reminding pros-
pective visitors that Shetland's rainfall is only about half
that of the rainiest parts of the West Highlands and that
Shetland, despite the very occasional 'spate', is not so
inhospitable as to lay on incessant rain just in the month
when most English visitors arrive.

Possibly preoccupation with the weather is even more marked in Shetland than it is elsewhere in the British Isles, and Shetlanders, constantly in sight of enormous expanses of sky, have a better opportunity than most to read the prospects in 'weather-heads' and other phenomena. Many old men could provide reliable forecasts without even a barometer. Nowadays, although the weather has less influence on everyday life, through its effects on communications and on the crops growing on the rigs, than it used to have, the interest seems to be as keen as ever. Men talk knowledgeably about 'highs' and 'lows' and 'anti-cyclones', but a lot of them still read the sea and the sky. I was amused to learn, shortly after I moved to my present home in Dysart, where I have almost as extensive a panorama of sea and sky as one would have in Shetland, that a neighbour, herself a native of Shetland, remarked, with more perception than strict accuracy, 'Anyone can see he's a Shetlander, the way he goes out to the corner of the house and lets his eyes range round the sea and the sky'.

6 ≣ The Kirk and the Community

Hamnavoe in South Yell was, like many another Shetland township, dominated physically by the parish church. A plain rectangle of 1838, rising in all its starkness from level ground in a treeless landscape, it seemed massive in relation to all the houses in the vicinity and it was a long way from any structures other than houses. The commercial centres — if one can call them so — with shops, post offices and the means of transport to and from other parts of Shetland, were at Burravoe and Ulsta, two miles or more to east and west respectively. Burravoe contained also the only large houses in the district, including the Manor House; and two other churches, an Episcopalian and a Methodist, were likewise a Burravoe. Even the manse for the parish church was at Burravoe. The somewhat isolated situation of the church was an inheritance from the middle ages, for it was on the site of a pre-reformation church — one of three in Yell — which had fallen into ruin by the end of the eighteenth century. In Mid Yell and North Yell the old sites were abandoned, leaving the walls of the old church in the midst of the graveyard, but in South Yell when the 1838 church was planned all efforts to find a different site had failed, and when a new manse was built in 1937 efforts to place it nearer the church were equally unsuccessful. The church was indeed central to the parish of South Yell, which included West Yell (though not East Yell), but it stood at the very extremity of the fifty or so houses which were spread out almost continuously, croft by croft, from

Neepaback, two and a half miles to the east; while to the west, except for lonely Arisdale, there was a stretch of uninhabited country. It could hardly have been less convenient and more discouraging, especially before there was mechanical transport. Yet, while the core of the usual Sunday morning congregation was drawn mainly from Hamnavoe, Houlland and Littlester (all within a mile or so), others 'traivelled' faithfully from farther afield. Not a great many came 'from west', but there would be one or two from Ulsta and sometimes from West Yell. The latter area had a United Free Church, and the local people, with the characteristic Shetland freedom from sectarian prejudice, were apt to attend it; on the other hand, if there was no service in Hamnavoe, my host and I sometimes 'traivelled' to attend a service in West Yell. Members of the parish church who resided in Copister were not so very far away as the crow flies, but the road, via Ulsta, was a long three miles. However, there were short-cuts for anyone on foot — and all were on foot in those days — between Copister and the Kirk, for it was possible to take to 'the hill'. At the mouth of the Arisdale Burn there were stepping-stones ('The Copister folk's stepping-stones'), but it was possible to do even better than that if an ebb tide left the head of Hamnavoe almost dry. Then it was practicable to 'win ower wi' da ebb' from the point of Saltness, and cousins of mine from Copister would set out for the Kirk in their rubber boots, carrying their shoes, and then, when they reached the road near the kirk, they left their boots by the roadside and donned their shoes.

Not the least difficulty in getting to the church was that experienced by the minister, whose manse was 2½ miles away but who had a greater obligation than his flock had to turn up regularly, regardless of the weather. In 'Mr Watson's time' (the ministry of the Rev John Watson, 1876-1914, which far exceeded in length that of any of his successors), the minister had a pony and trap, and the corrugated iron hut erected for the shelter of his pony during services still stands just outside the kirk-yard-dyke. Some of his successors walked, as his predecessors had no doubt done. Mr Douglas Beck (1935-40) was the first minister to have a car, but Mr Bert McLaughlan (1929-31) had had a motor-bike, and brought his wife (who generally played the organ) on his pillion. I remember him turning up in oilskins on a stormy morning and mounting the pulpit steps in his rubber boots.

All in all there was usually a fair congregation at both services (12 noon and 6 p.m.) on a fine Sunday. The younger people tended to turn out especially for the evening service, after which they paired off to walk the roads for an hour or two. The bell was rung for a minute or two a quarter of an hour before the start of the service and again just before the minister was ready to enter the pulpit. People generally arrived in good time, and the men usually congregated outside and chatted for a few minutes before going in to settle in their pews. In the actual conduct of the service I saw few differences from what I was accustomed to in Presbyterian churches in the south, but it was the habit, after a psalm or hymn was announced, for the organist to play over the tune and then the minister to read the first verse before singing started — this was a reversal of the order I was familiar with. The other unusual feature was the survival of the practice of using ladles to take up the collection. The lighting in the church was by paraffin lamps, and I well remember when the much improved pressure lamps, the Tilleys, took the place of the older variety with their wicks. In winter times the lamps were lit even in good daylight because there was no other form of heating and they did a little to lift the chill.

The Shetland talent and enthusiasm for music found some expression and outlet in the work of the choir,

43 Mid Yell 1931

44 Mid Yell 1982

45 Heilinabretta, Fetlar

46   At Muness Castle 1935

47   On a basking shark 1929

48   Brough Lodge about 1930

49   Brough Lodge 1982

50 'Dreepie Nose'

51 White Hill of Gossabrough

52 Horse of Burravoe

53 Graveland: Ern Stack in middle distance

54 The rugged cloven peak of the Ern Stack: Ramna Stacks behind

55 Under the 'Easter Banks'

56   The stacks of the Stuis

whose older members, at least, had been drilled in part-singing while they were at school and had learned to read their parts (usually from sol-fa). The choir had practices on a week-day evening, at least before an occasion like the Harvest Festival, when some quite ambitious settings were prepared, and at the practices there was a fair attendance of young and old, male and female.

The Kirk had had an organ or harmonium since 1902, and one had been presented by Mrs Turnbull, wife of the local proprietor, in 1911. Local musical skill extended to instrumental as well as vocal music, and although the fiddle was the favourite, there were many people, and members of one family in particular, who seemed able to turn their hands to any instrument. But not all of those who could play a keyboard instrument were willing to perform in church, though good service was given by some local women who had either overcome their nervousness or were unable to resist pressure. I was foolish enough to admit that I could make noises on an organ and — incredible as it now seems — for some years I quite frequently acted as organist. It was an inspiring experience for me, and I could only hope that the precision and efficiency of the choir concealed the erratic and disagreeable sounds which surely sometimes came from the organ. Curiously enough — and I have always regarded it as one of my distinctions, because one is apt to be especially proud of achievements which have nothing to do with one's professional work — I even acted as organist on the first known occasion when a Moderator of the General Assembly, the Rt. Rev P. D. Thompson, preached in Hamnavoe Kirk, on 22nd July 1934. (Oddly enough, though it should not be mentioned in the same breath except to bring out a contrast rather than a similarity, my predecessor as Professor and as Historiographer, Robert Kerr Hannay, was a very capable organist who was known to play in the Church of St Giles in Edinburgh, an event which the beadle thought

as deserving of a commemorative plaque as some of the
subjects of the tablets in that church.) The occasions when
I believe I was able to do a real service were funerals, for
it was then clearly understood that no woman could
attend a funeral service and there would have been no
music without my poor efforts. So far as I am aware, no
one ever stayed away from the Kirk because I was
performing. In this respect I had a different experience
many years later in the Episcopal Church at Burravoe.
After there ceased to be a resident parson there, the
Bishop of Aberdeen and Orkney thought it might be a
good idea to licence me as a lay reader so that I could take
services occasionally. But alas! when I was duly
advertised to officiate no one came. I do not blame them:
they heard enough from Gordon Donaldson without
going to church to hear him. 'A prophet is not without
honour, save in his own country'. And, by one of those
coincidences which the lectionary throws up not
infrequently, that sentence was in one of the lessons
when, on an earlier occasion, I had preached in the
Episcopal Church and there had been a congregation.

Funerals were — and still are — occasions when the
kirk was very visibly the centre of the community. The
tradition was to gather at the deceased's home, possibly
some miles away, and the coffin was brought out and laid
on chairs — which were upset when the coffin was
removed from them, because of a belief that otherwise
there would be another death in the house within a year.
An impressive and moving procession then started for the
kirk. The coffin was carried on hand-spikes, and from the
long train of mourners one group after another subtly
moved forward to take their turn in this duty. Oddly
enough I do not recall ever being at a wedding in South
Yell — though I was at one in Mid Yell. Marriages in
church seem in those days to have been exceptional, and
there was, besides, a strong tendency, even between the
Wars, to go to Lerwick to be married.

There was a Sunday School, which, unlike those in the south, met in the summer months, and it was held after the morning service. I knew little of this at first hand, though I once did fill a gap when the minister was not available; I think it was on the occasion when the Moderator preached and had to go on elsewhere immediately after the service. My recollection is that the Sunday School itself was quite well attended, but the 'Sunday School Picnic' was one of the great occasions of the year, to which as many adults as children seemed to come, from every part of the parish. In 1930 (when I think it was something new) it was held in the Ness of Galtagarth, but thereafter it was usually in the 'Holy Hole' beside the Hamnavoe Burn. This was a natural amphitheatre where, it was said, open-air services had been held in the period between the final abandonment of the ancient church and the erection of the new one in 1838, and it had a suitable eminence in the middle called 'The Pulpit Knowe'. This oval mound, I always suspected, had been a Norse grave (and someone did say that if I dug there I would find 'deid men's banes') and that this had made the site 'Holy' in far earlier days.

While Sunday services, funerals and the Sunday School Picnic put the Kirk firmly in its place as the focus of the community, what proportion of the people it influenced in their faith and life it would, as always, be hard to say. There was a goodly number of deeply committed Christians, there was an element of the evangelical fervour associated with so many coastal communities, and there was only one militant and vocal atheist. I recall one relevant remark — but this was in Mid Yell. With two or three other people, I was passing the manse, and some comment was made about the minister's stipend, which at that time was £400 per annum (which seemed a lot in a community where money was little used). 'Ay, four hundred a year just for flytin' apo' the deevil twa 'oors o' a Sunday'. But it was not unkindly meant. And it should be said that precious little of the stipend derived from the local congregation, for the level of giving still reflected the older dispensation whereby the stipend and the upkeep of church and manse had been the responsibility of the heritors alone, so that what went into the plate, or rather ladle, had been simply by way of alms for the poor. This system had ceased to operate in 1926, but it still coloured the popular attitude in the 1930s. Now, after another fifty years, it has been generally forgotten that for centuries the whole expense of church, manse, stipend, school, schoolhouse and teacher's salary was no charge on tenants but was shouldered by the lairds alone.

There were certainly many who showed little outward sign of a lively interest in the church and its mission. But they did not like this to be said, and I once got into hot water on the issue. *The Weekly Scotsman* had printed an article of a type which was and is all too common, in which a journalist with superficial knowledge writes nonsense about Shetland, confident that he is not likely to be contradicted and that people will believe anything about such an outlandish place. In this instance, he had stated that the people were all Presbyterians, that Bible-reading and family worship were habitual, and so on. I rushed in with youthful impetuosity and arrogance, in a note published on 16th January 1937. I pointed out that other denominations besides Presbyterians were represented, that my only experience of family worship had been with cousins who were Plymouth Brethren, that I had seen little Bible-reading and that the knowledge of scripture was no more extensive than it was generally in Scotland or England. Not content with explaining in detail how the writer was wrong, I made a fatal generalisation that 'many families cannot be said to have any church connection. There are places where church-going is the exception rather than the rule'. The next letter I had from Shetland was written in anger rather than in sorrow. 'Where', I was asked, 'are the families with no church connection? How did I know that people did not read a chapter of the Bible night and morning?' But in that unlucky note in *The Weekly Scotsman* I made some other comments which are perhaps worth repeating. 'Some of the ideas and practices associated with Scottish Presbyterianism do not appear to have made headway in Shetland, which never adopted the ruling of the Scottish reformed kirk on church festivals. Christmas, particularly, has retained a place there which it does not have on the mainland of Scotland. The crofters regard Christmas Day as a day on which no work except what is absolutely necessary may be done. No woman would think of knitting, for instance. Presbyterians complain that their church ought to, but does not, give them services on Christmas Day. A second notable survival from pre-Presbyterian times is the custom of praying for the dead. Usually the prayer is a brief, formal phrase — "God rest him" or something like that — but I once heard a more specific petition from the pulpit of a parish church, the preacher being a layman of Shetland birth'.

Faith and superstition are very different things, but there were superstitions which had a religious origin. For many generations the disease of scrofula, or tuberculosis of certain glands, could, so it was believed, be cured by the royal touch, and it was known as 'The King's Evil'. It was in the seventeenth century that this superstition was most prevalent, and it reached its climax under Charles II (1660-85). There is probably no other person to whom so many miracles have been ascribed. In a single year Charles performed the ceremony of 'touching for the Evil' no less than 8500 times, and in the course of his reign he is said to have 'touched' nearly 100,000 of his subjects. When the crown went to the house of Hanover, and the direct line of succession was broken, the notion that kings inherited a miraculous power had to be given up. The Stewarts in exile, indeed, continued to touch for

the Evil, and the old ceremony was revived when Bonnie
Prince Charlie was in Edinburgh in 1745. But sufferers
from scrofula who could no longer find a remedy in the
royal touch sought a new cure. Material objects had
already been used in place of the king's touch. After
Charles I's execution it was found that handkerchiefs
dipped in his blood possessed the same efficacy as his
living hand, and hundreds of people were said to have
benefited in this way. Besides, when the ceremony of
touching was performed with due formality, the king had
usually hung round the necks of the sufferers gold pieces
coined for the purpose. It may therefore have seemed
logical that ordinary coins, bearing the imprint of the
king, would be of use. This belief, the latest form of the
ancient superstition, lingered in most of the country
districts of Britain until last century. In Shetland,
scrofula, known as 'The Cruels', was very common, and
coins of the various Stewart sovereigns were kept to be
employed as remedies. At one time there were probably
one or two in every parish, and many of them were used
within living memory. I had first-hand knowledge of one
such coin, an English half-crown of Charles II, dated
1672. It has been handed down in a family for at least
four generations, and in spite of its age careful treatment
had preserved it in excellent condition. When anyone was
affected by scrofula, this 'Cruel Coin' was sent for. To
have effect, it had to be used by the third son or third
daughter in a family and it was applied to the wound on
three successive mornings while the person using it was
fasting. The last occasion of its use seems to have been
about 1902 or 1903, when it was applied by a little girl, a
third daughter. The 'patient' of that time told me of it
when she was a woman of about eighty, and recollected
little of the occurrence, but was confident that the coin
was effective as a cure. It can have done no harm, for she
lived until 1942, when she was 93. The coin is still
preserved, and quite recently, on the death of its previous

holder (a third daughter) it was handed on to her third son.

I was told of one case of witchcraft dating from about the same early years of this century. An old woman was observed scraping some paint, or possibly tar, from a boat which had been successful at the fishing and transferring it to another craft, in the hope, presumably, of 'taking the profit' from one boat and giving it to another.

The Kirk was always there, operating weekly and at least typifying the fellowship of the community. It was not so long since the church had still been the only public building in the parish, as had been true for centuries, and it had been used for 'soirées' as well as more sacred purposes. There was, however, even when I first knew Shetland, a public hall in most areas, the place of meeting for more secular activities, among which 'the Dance' was the most frequent. Concerts were for special occasions, such as a Regatta Day, but a Dance, it seemed, might be put on at almost any time whenever a few active spirits were prepared to arrange one. And little arrangement was required: fiddlers could be counted on to be present, the harmonium could be trundled along from the Episcopal Church, and two or three 'cooks' were found who had little to do except to brew tea. The dances were very energetic affairs, devoted largely to the old-fashioned square dances — Quadrilles, Lancers and Reels, and only an occasional schottische, waltz, one-step or two-step. Undoubtedly the appeal lay in the rhythmic movements, carried out with the utmost vigour. As spirits rose there would be a cry, 'Shake her up, boys' or 'Open up the floor', the later an exhortation, in Quadrilles, to extend the movements of the figure to the whole floor and not confine it to a single set of eight. The start was late — long after the advertised time, when no one had turned up — and, fortified at intervals by strong tea and buns, it was possible to carry on well into the morning. It was rare in pre-war days for any liquid other than tea to be much

in evidence at an ordinary dance in South Yell. The other
break, besides tea, came when the Tilley lamps were
taken down from their hooks and pumped up afresh.

The great annual event was the Regatta, much more
than a series of sailing races, which after all engaged
relatively few men. There were land sports, rowing races
and, to wind up, a concert and dance. The series of
regattas at Mid Yell, Cullivoe and Uyeasound were the
landmarks in the social calendar for the North Isles at the
height of the summer. In South Yell, as it happened,
regattas were very rare for a number of years, and the
only one I was associated with was in 1934 — that year of
years.

It was the first season of my outboard, and it was
obvious that my boat, being the only powered boat in the
area, would be used to lay the buoys. On the day before
the regatta I was to take the boat along to Burravoe.
Johnnie came down to the banks to help me off, and as
the wind was steadily freshening he remarked, 'It's just
enough wind for you to go to Burravoe wi'.' It was a
south-wester, raising the worst chop I had encountered to
date, and I was a bit apprehensive going round the point
of Burraness and entering Greenholm Sound (where, to
make matters worse, my tiller-extension snapped off). By
the time I got to the Brough pier I had had enough and it
was agreed that we would postpone the buoy-laying until
the following morning. My boat was loaded up with the
gear and laid off at Overby. Next morning I started from
Hamnavoe at six, to walk to Brough and be there before
seven. The wind had gone down overnight (as is the way
of westerly winds) and the buoys were laid without
difficulty. After that I was involved in starting the sailing
race and lending my boat for a pulling race (by which
time the wind had freshened again from the south-west
and was blowing right into the voe, with the result that
the competitor in my boat, who had been so confident of
her, got only a second). There were land sports to follow,

then back on foot to Hamnavoe to dress for the concert (in
which I took part in a sketch) and dance, and did not get
home until six a.m. — the only time I recall doing a
twenty-four hour day. A day or two later Robbie
Hughson and I made the round of the sailing course once
more and lifted the buoys.

Johnnie's concern when I left for Burravoe on that
Regatta day had not been unjustified, for it had indeed
proved that there was rather too much wind for me to go
to Burravoe with in any comfort that day. There was less
justification in another remark made one evening when I
was leaving Gossabrough for Hamnavoe. There was a
visitor in the house who knew neither me, nor my boat
nor my engine, and he said 'If you're going for
Hamnavoe tonight, then if you've any money you better
make a will and leave it to me'.

The other great annual event, besides a Regatta, was
the Show — the Agricultural Show — but it was a great
deal more than that. It had a wider constituency than a
Regatta, for while there were half a dozen regattas in
different places in Unst and Yell there was only one show
in each island (as well as one in Fetlar). It was a busy time
for exhibitors, and as the show was usually followed by a
sale, there was a big movement of animals from all parts
of the island to the showground, which in Yell was at
Windhouse, half way between Mid Yell and Westsandwick and as central as any spot could be. Many went
who had no great interest in the prize-winning
capabilities of animals or produce or hosiery, for the show
was a great social occasion, where one met people whom,
in the days when there was little public transport, one
might seldom see at any other time in the year. It was at a
show that I first had a talk with that remarkable man
Laurence Williamson, for whom the crowd at Windhouse
provided a splendid opportunity for his careful
observation of the physical characteristics of his fellows
and the deductions he could draw from them. As we

K

chatted, his eyes were constantly ranging around, and
from time to time he would comment on some resemblance which indicated a relationship or some feature
which pointed to a more (or less) pure Scandinavian
ancestry. A good many people went from Yell to the
Fetlar show, which always had a high reputation both for
the quality of the animals raised in that fertile island
(where, I remarked, the cattle grazed on land which in
Yell would have been mown for hay) and where visitors
knew they would have a warm welcome from people who
were exceptionally kind and hospitable even by Shetland
standards. A show, like a regatta, was followed by a
concert and dance.

7 ≡ 'The Steamers' and 'The Mail'

A Shetland without air transport, without broadcasting, without a telephone link to the mainland of Great Britain or even among all the islands, let alone to the rest of the world — all that is remote from the minds of a generation which has now reached maturity and is verging on middle age. Yet that was Shetland as I first knew it. True, there was the link of the telegraph, but it was a link that was visibly tenuous — those two frail wires running along the road in Yell and the single line continuing to Unst. Besides, the submarine cables which linked Shetland to Scotland (and also to Iceland) were liable to break: in mid-winter 1931-32 the direct cable to Aberdeen and the indirect cable via Orkney, as well as the North Isles cable, were all out of action. And, the telegraph apart, communication and transport of all kinds, whether of people, mails, goods, news and the written and printed word, depended almost exclusively on 'the steamers'.

Between the Wars there were three regular passenger sailings every week in winter, each leaving Leith in an afternoon or evening. The 'weekend boat' left on Thursday for Aberdeen, Kirkwall and Lerwick, where she arrived some time after mid-day on Saturday. The 'west side boat', on Sunday, called at Aberdeen and Stromness and reached Scalloway on Tuesday, often going on to other west side ports. The 'direct boat' sailed from Leith on Tuesday for Aberdeen and Lerwick, arriving early on Thursday morning. The departures from Shetland were on Monday, Wednesday and Friday

evenings. In summer, however, there were five steamers
each week. The 'weekend boat' and the 'west side boat'
retained the same schedules as in winter, but there was a
secondary Kirkwall boat leaving Leith on Tuesday to
arrive in Lerwick on Thursday afternoon and leave again
early on Friday morning, and the direct boat made a
double run, one from Leith on Monday morning calling
at Aberdeen and arriving in Lerwick on Tuesday about
mid-day and leaving for Aberdeen on Wednesday at
noon, and a second from Aberdeen on Thursday at
2 p.m. and leaving Lerwick on Saturday evening to
arrive in Aberdeen on Sunday morning and Leith on
Sunday evening. There were always people on the pier at
Lerwick to welcome a steamer and to see her off —
except, indeed, on Friday at 4 a.m. (later 2 a.m.) — and
the outstanding occasion was Saturday evening, when the
direct boat was leaving and the weekend boat arriving.

The bulk of the normal passenger traffic was on the
direct boat and the weekend boat, but as all the services
carried not only passengers but also freight and mails,
their times of arrival and departure were matters of
concern to most people, at least in Lerwick. The window
of the North of Scotland Company's office on the
Esplanade displayed helpful notices of the times of
departure of north-bound steamers: e.g. 'S.S. *St. Magnus*
left Kirkwall for Lerwick at 5.45 a.m.' This gave some
idea of the ship's likely time of arrival, for the benefit of
those who were expecting goods, intending to meet a
passenger or awaiting the delivery of mail. Such notices
were indispensable, not only because the small steamers
of those days were liable to be held up by heavy weather
and, before the days of radar, could be seriously delayed
by fog, but also because the posted times of departure
were never adhered to. A ship due to leave Aberdeen for
Lerwick at 11 a.m. might leave at any time between
11.10 and 1.30. If one had seen the notice giving the
actual hour of departure one had a fair idea when the boat

could be expected, and in due course she indicated her arrival in the harbour with the familiar long and short blasts on her steam whistle, which penetrated all over Lerwick and beyond. There could, indeed, be a false alarm. One foggy Friday morning, when the *St. Sunniva,* on the direct run, was late, the sound of the usual whistle brought people hastening down to the pier, only to find that the arrival was the little cargo vessel *St. Fergus.*

The same uncertainty surrounded the hour of departure from Lerwick. Often as a result of awaiting the arrival of the North Isles steamer, which, especially in the lamb-shipping season, could be hours late, the south boat might be long detained. As long as she was working, all over Lerwick one heard the clatter of the steam cranes, and in due course her impending departure was announced stage by stage with the ringing of the three bells, one about half an hour before she was expected to leave, the second perhaps ten minutes before, and the third when she was at last ready to cast off. There was no need to leave the house for the pier until the first bell went. Then we would come from the Hillhead down one of the lanes. My favourite, as long as the steamers lay at Victoria Pier, was Bank Lane, which provided the best view of the ship at her berth, and when I use that lane now my thoughts go back over the many ships — fifteen in all, I reckon — which I have seen there over the years.

All this preoccupation with 'the steamers' was something I inherited, for it was passed on to me by my father. Even before I ever set off for Shetland I had been aboard North of Scotland ships in Leith Docks and had heard of their reputations and history. They have been part of my life as long as I can remember, and the family was always up to date with news about them. It was characteristic of the general atmosphere of trust that there was not in those days any forbidding notice 'No Admittance except on Business', and one strolled casually on to and around the ships as they lay at Leith. I recall the humiliation I felt on the occasion — some years after

World War II — when, for the first time, I was
challenged with 'What do you want here?' when I walked
up the gangway of the *St. Magnus* (III) one Sunday.

While the schedule was almost unaltered throughout
the whole inter-war period, the fleet changed con-
siderably. In the early 1920s not one of the vessels
exceeded approximately 1000 tons, the *St. Ninian* was of
only 700 tons and the veteran *St. Clair,* built in 1868 and
of only 630 tons, continued to face the winter Atlantic on
the west side until 1936. The third *St. Magnus,* of 1924, at
1500 tons, was such a startling change that it was hardly
surprising that she was described as 'mair laek a peerie
liner'. I still remember the impression made on me, when
I first boarded her, by her spacious dining saloon and
long wide alleyways — though no doubt they would seem
cramped enough nowadays and I recall how small she
looked in her final years. As with other ships after her and
no doubt before her, heads were at first shaken over her
bulk and her superstructure — 'too much top-hamper' —
but before her career ended in 1960 she had earned
recognition as 'a splendid sea-boat' and she seemed to
epitomise solidity and reliability. I think she was above all
others my favourite main-line ship or 'south boat' and I
made many voyages in her. I have almost complete recall
of the first voyage I made in her, going south in 1929 and
immensely enjoying the leisured progress by way of
Kirkwall and Aberdeen. One stood behind the glass
panels at the forward end of the boat deck to watch the
scenery coming up after the departures from Lerwick and
Kirkwall and on the approach to Aberdeen, and on the
long day between Kirkwall and Aberdeen one lay in a
deck-chair on the after-deck watching the mast-tops
swaying gently against the sky.

The direct boat when I made my earliest visits was
the first *St. Sunniva* (864 tons), originally built as a steam
yacht for cruises to Norway in 1887 and converted in
1908 for the direct run, with cargo and mails. Though

with her fine lines she can never have been the steadiest of
ships, the quality of her accommodation was above
average and, while in her later years she never did the 16
knots she had attained in her cruising days, she could
make smart passages. Her last skipper was 'Bonnie
Willie' Williamson, whose pride in his ship was paralleled
by his showmanship. On a Monday morning, shortly
before the ship's departure from Leith, a taxi drew up at
the foot of the gangway and Captain Williamson, with
waxed moustache and immaculate white gloves,
emerged, to make his way to the bridge where, it was
remarked, he strutted about like a peacock. There was a
lot of ritual in those days which later disappeared: when a
ship berthed, the purser was always standing ready to go
ashore, the ship's papers grasped importantly in his hand,
and when the gangway was in position he was the first to
set foot on it and step briskly down to make his way to the
office. I went north and south on the *St. Sunniva* in 1922
and north on her in 1929; it was only on my way south in
the latter year that I discovered the joys of the *St. Magnus*.
Captain Williamson's fondness for smart passages may
have been his undoing, for the *St. Sunniva* was wrecked on
Mousa early in the morning on 10th April 1930. Her loss
— the first in peace-time since that of the *St. Nicholas* in
1914 and the first ever on the Shetland coast — was a
shock. I was on holiday in Rothesay at the time and well
remember seeing the bill outside a newsagent's shop,
'Scottish Mailboat wrecked' and going in to find on the
front page a picture of the familiar *St. Sunniva* half-
submerged. The event brought out the weakness in
Shetland's communications, for her S.O.S. was picked
up by the coast radio station at Wick but, as there was no
telephone to Shetland, the message could not be received
there until the telegraph office opened. It also emphasised
the need for a lifeboat in Shetland (though all the *St.
Sunniva's* passengers and crew had been safely taken
ashore in her own boats), but a more cogent argument to

that end was the appalling tragedy, a few days earlier, of
the trawler *Ben Doran,* mentioned in chapter 2. Lerwick
got its lifeboat later in the same year — a useful fact to
keep in mind when dating photographs of the town's
waterfront.

The advent of the second *St. Sunniva,* launched a year
all but a few days from the loss of the first, occasioned
great excitement and speculation, if only because Lerwick
always had an especially proprietary feeling towards the
direct boat. It was not quite true, as was rumoured, that
she was to be 'board for board' a replica of her predecessor, but she was essentially a larger version, with
even more extreme lines, and it was a remarkable
achievement to incorporate in such a vision of beauty the
utilitarian needs of the passenger, mail, cargo and
livestock trade. She was not unreasonably criticised by
some for being altogether too conservative in design, and
the late Sheriff Wallace pronounced her 'obsolete from
the day she was launched'. Besides, her shapely hull
made her extremely lively. It was said — but so many
things were said about 'the steamers' that one almost
hesitates to pass them on — that after her first encounter
with heavy weather Captain William Gifford flatly
refused to take her to sea again until more ballast had
been put in; and it is a fact that one friend of mine, who
had been trained in sail, remarked after travelling in her
that he was startled to find how she heeled over under
wind pressure. Critics showed some prescience, for the
ship met her end when she turned turtle on service as a
rescue ship with a transatlantic convoy in 1943. On the
other hand, she received a testimonial from a member of
the crew, Jimmie Scollay, whom I knew well. One bad
night, when they had been plugging into a head sea,
Captain Gifford remarked to him that it must have been
very uncomfortable in the crew's quarters down in the
foc'sle, but the reply came, 'Oh, man, she's just like a
feather bed'. By the time the second *St. Sunniva* appeared

in 1931 I was completely obsessed by anything to do with
Shetland and was as excited as anybody about the new
steamer. It so happened that as I went north in the spring
that year I was in Aberdeen the day before she was
launched, and I was able to take two photographs of her
on the stocks. To my delight and amazement I discovered
— what none of the reports had mentioned — that her
hull was painted white. When I came south a fortnight
later I photographed her in the fitting-out berth. She
started her first run to Lerwick from Aberdeen on
Monday, 1st June, and was not in Leith until the
following Sunday, 7th June. There was always a crowd of
the Edinburgh Shetland community on the wharf on a
Sunday evening to 'meet the boat', and it was an
uncommonly large crowd that welcomed the beautiful
new ship. I saw the *St. Sunniva* for the last time when I
went south on her in August 1939, a fortnight before the
outbreak of war. On the following Sunday word arrived
that she had been requisitioned, as part of the preparation
for naval operations.

There was less excitement about the next new
steamer — which turned out to be the last steamer in the
literal sense of the word — the second *St. Clair,* in 1937,
because she was destined for service on the west side in
summer and the weekend run in winter, though she
became the direct boat after the war (1946-60). I was a
London student when she came into service, but I
happened to be in Edinburgh for the Easter vacation
when she made her first appearance in Leith and I
remember going on board to see a layout which, for the
North boats, was revolutionary, for it departed from the
tradition of the second-class accommodation forward and
the dining saloon aft. She was the only ship which I saw
on both her first and her last appearances in Leith, for I
was there to see this last of the steamships when she
arrived from Aberdeen on her way to the breaker's yard
on 1st April 1967.

It was a great joy in 1945, when I made my first post-war visit to Shetland, to board once more the familiar *St. Magnus* (III), then on the direct run. The war in Europe had finished only a few weeks before, and when I went north the ship was still sailing under emergency rules, with the boats swung out when whe was at sea. This meant of course that the boat deck and promenade deck were closed to passengers, but of this I was not aware and, while we still were tied up at Aberdeen, I went up the companion-way as usual to the forward end of the boat deck, to encounter an irate Captain Macmillan, 'Don't you know there's no passengers allowed on this deck? Can't you read the notice?' As I retreated, I saw that there was in truth a somewhat inconspicuous notice at the side of the companion-way. It was, I think, the only rebuke I have ever had from the master of a ship: I have remarked that I have never been reprimanded for going on to the navigation bridge but that in a recent year I was once reprimanded for *not* going up to pay a visit which had by that time become normal. When I returned from Shetland in 1945, three weeks later, conditions on the *St. Magnus* were getting back to normal.

After World War II the story of 'the steamers' (which latterly had no steam except in the galley) was one of curtailment and consolidation of services, as the aeroplanes took over more and more of the mail and passenger traffic. But there were still two Kirkwall boats in summer until 1967 and one for a few years more, offering a repetition of the old way of life. The direct boat, doing a double run all the year round, no longer came as of old to Leith, but one could still go down to the docks on a Saturday afternoon to welcome the second *St. Ninian* (of 1950) when she arrived from Lerwick, Kirkwall and Aberdeen. The direct run itself, first with the second *St. Clair* of 1937 and from 1960 to 1977 with the third *St. Clair,* became a model of efficiency and regularity. The ships now sailed precisely on time, and, with their reserves of speed as well as their greater size and their equipment with radar, were able to adhere to standard passage-times unless in exceptional weather.

I liked the third *St. Clair,* perhaps partly because she had, unlike the second, been built for the direct run and spent her whole career on it. As I was in Shetland very frequently while she was in service, I think I probably made more passages on her than on any other of the main line ships, and she lives in my memory very vividly. It was on her, oddly enough, that I made my longest trip from Aberdeen to Lerwick, when I went north for Up-Helly-Aa in 1961 — thirty-six hours on board from pier to pier. That sounds formidable, but twenty-four of the thirty-six were spent at anchor in Lerwick harbour; we had come north with a southerly gale — very comfortably thanks to the stabilisers — but at Lerwick we could not take the pier. It was by no means an unpleasant experience. Even more memorable were another thirty-six hours I spent on the vessel when, as the guest of the Company after I had written *Northwards by Sea,* I made a trip from Aberdeen to Troon when the *St. Clair* went for her annual overhaul. It was my only experience of a 3000-ton private yacht, and the voyage was an unusual one in many ways. There was a full-scale north-westerly storm, the full force of which we encountered when we rounded Buchan Ness, and off Rattray Head she was practically beaten to a standstill: in one hour she did only 3½ miles, and Captain Ramsay remarked that he simply could not get Rattray off the radar screen. We lost eight hours between that point and Duncansby Head, but this had the fortunate result that we were off Cape Wrath at 8 a.m. and not at midnight, giving us a splendid view of that headland in rough conditions. Once round that 'turning point', as the Norsemen christened it, we had a following wind, and drove down the Minches under brilliant conditions. On that trip I occupied berth No. 68. I may have been in it before, but I was in it so often later that

the stewardess could not dissociate me from it, and on one
occasion when I did happen to be elsewhere she, by force
of habit, put my evening milk and sandwiches, which
were a standing order, into 68 and discovered her mistake
only when I rang from the cabin I was in. (Cabin service,
which was such an agreeable feature of the ships,
disappeared with the advent of the present, fourth, *St.
Clair*.)

In my earlier years, and even until a considerable
time after World War II, it was far from common to see
vehicles being carried on any of the steamers. When they
did appear, they were usually carried on deck, and
naturally were noticeable. But the carrying of cars
increased as car ownership spread, and the third *St. Clair*,
although she had no special accommodation for the
purpose, generally had in summer her full complement of
thirty-odd cars. The skill in loading and unloading the
vehicles improved immensely over the years, and drivers
in time ceased to regard the process as a major hazard. I
had no temptation to take my own car north until there
was a vehicle ferry to Yell, but once that appeared I twice
took my car on the third *St. Clair*, and I remembered to
photograph the car being hoisted aboard in the old way
when I did this for the last time. The fourth *St. Clair*, a
drive-through car-carrier, at last made it possible to drive
all the way from Edinburgh to Yell — a thing that would
have been regarded as a wild dream sixty years ago.

The interest of Lerwick in 'the steamers', great
though it was, was surpassed by that of the North Isles
folk in 'the steamer' — the first *Earl of Zetland* from 1877
to 1946 and the second until 1975 — for it constituted for
all the islands the main, and for some the only, regular
link with the rest of the world. The mail, the movement of
people, supplies to the local shops, were all dependent on
'the steamer'. Few questions can have been more often
asked than the question, 'Are ye been awar' o' da
steamer?' It is no accident that in my *Northwards by Sea* the

longest chapter is that on 'The North Isles of Shetland', and I would not repeat all the reminiscences I set down there. Nor would I encroach on the field of Mr Adam Robson, who has written with such affection and understanding of the old *Earl*. And yet there is plenty more to tell.

Spending most of my time in South Yell I was very well placed strategically to watch 'the steamer's' movements. She called at Burravoe on both her North Isles run and her Yell Sound run, and it was not rare for her to be in Burravoe six days in the week. But that apart, she could be seen from the Yell hills or cliffs when she was on other parts of her travels — coming north from Whalsay, heading out to Skerries, between Mid Yell and Brough Lodge, crossing Yell Sound, making special calls in the lamb-shipping season. Some of her many calls at Burravoe were unscheduled, and not even covered by the phrase '(when required)' which appeared against the names of some ports in the time-tables. The old *Earl,* or rather her genial skipper William Spence, was extremely obliging and it was almost as casual as stopping a bus. I remember going aboard the *Earl* at Lerwick on a Friday morning before she sailed and finding the captain seated reading outside his cabin, to ask him if he would call at Burravoe when I went north on Sunday. 'Oh, we'll call', came the ready answer. Of course when she was on passage between Whalsay and Mid Yell it was hardly out of her way to stop at the mouth of Burra Voe. But I always liked to have a run out to Skerries, and I would go aboard in Burravoe to ask if she would call for me on Monday when she was scheduled to proceed from Mid Yell to Skerries. Even this Spence obligingly did, though latterly he was under some constraint: 'They said that when I was going to Skerries I wasn't to call at Burravoe for one passenger. It's half an hour's steaming'. However, Peter Williamson wanted to ship lambs from Burravoe on that particular Monday, and that made the call possible. It was not, I think, until after World War II that it became the rule that all applications for special calls had to go through the Lerwick office. I often wondered how Spence remembered all he had undertaken to do. It was perhaps more difficult to ensure that the ports were notified and had a flitboat ready. I once thought I was in trouble. In order to have a weekend in Unst I went north on the steamer when she made her scheduled call at Burravoe on Friday, and, as I intimated that I would be coming back on Monday, it was agreed that she would call at Burravoe that day, when her schedule was Mid Yell - Skerries. After we left Mid Yell on the Monday, Davie Gray, the purser, came up to me and said, 'Do you think they know at Burravoe that we're going to call?' I had to admit that I was just assuming that they knew — and after all the *Earl* had been there on Saturday and probably on Sunday, so the word could have been passed on. The purser on his side admitted that if he had thought about it earlier he could have sent a wire from Mid Yell. Hoping for the best, when we were off the Horse of Burravoe Spence gave two blasts on the whistle (the recognised sign that he was calling at Burravoe but no going into the voe), then another two blasts when we were at the back of Heoganess. Even so, when we rounded the point of the ness and came in sight of the pier there was still no sign of life. Yet another pair of 'toots' brought the merchant, Mackie Hughson, and one of his assistants, Robbie Bruce, running down the pier to cast off the small boat which always lay afloat there. So we were saved from being carried on to Lerwick. It should be mentioned that a notice on the steamer stated firmly that the Company took no responsibility for boating between ship and shore.

That was not a case of deliberate delay. In *Northwards by Sea* I mentioned the 'fascinating tactical battle' between the skipper of the *Earl*, trying to tempt the flitboat out, and the flitmen, lingering at the pier as long as was decently possible in the hope of tempting him a little bit farther in. But there was room for fine judgment. When the steamer first dropped anchor she might well be beam-to-wind, providing a lee side, whereas after she had settled to her anchor and came head-to-wind the sea was running along both sides. I recall one morning boarding the old *Earl* at Brough Lodge with a strong nor-wester laying right on to the shore, and encountering an irate Davie Gray, exclaiming, 'Why didn't you come off sooner? We were giving you some lee.' It did not always pay to be dilatory.

The only time I was in any way let down by the obliging steamer and her skipper was on the day of the Fetlar Show in 1934. I joined her at Burravoe early in the morning, about 7 a.m., whence she proceeded to Mid Yell and then Hubie. She left Hubie for her Yell Sound calls while we enjoyed the Fetlar Show. We had little idea when the *Earl* would return, and although we were ready for her from the early evening, it was 10.30 when she arrived and took us on board for Mid Yell. I wondered what would happen at this late hour, and on the passage to Mid Yell I observed the mate, the late Tommy Gifford, eyeing the passengers and considering their probable destinations. I knew well that I was the only passenger for Burravoe, and I heard him tell Captain Spence, 'There's the Donaldson boy'. Spence then came up to me and reported that 'Mackie said he wouldn't come off'. I confess I was a little doubtful about this, and Spence was not very explicit as to how he had heard from Mackie, for I was fairly confident that Mackie would have come off if the steamer had been willing to call. However, it was evident that I would be put ashore at Mid Yell. Tommy Gifford suggested that the policeman might lend me his bike — of which I had had experience before, as mentioned in chapter 2. This did not appeal, and I preferred to walk. I landed from the flitboat on the pier at Linkshouse at 11.45 p.m. and reached Hamnavoe (10½ miles away) at 2.30 a.m., of course following the road all the way. It was a fine fresh night, in the later part of August, but it was my most solitary walk ever — few cars on the road in those days even in the hours of daylight and none at all at night. Somewhere in East Yell I came on a group of ponies beside a peatstack and they sprang to life with a tremendous clatter which startled me.

When the steamer was not visible, she was frequently brought to mind by her penetrating 'toot', about which poets, or at any rate rhymesters, have rhapsodised and which, with a favourable wind, could be heard over very long distances in the prevailing silence. From South Yell I have heard her blowing in Symbister on her way north, but the fascinating thing was how one could trace her progress port by port as she proceeded beyond Burravoe. In the solitude of a walk in the Yell hills in a summer afternoon I heard her blow not only in Mid Yell but in Brough Lodge and Uyeasound, and on her Yell Sound runs one could hear the familiar sound going the rounds of Mossbank, Ollaberry, Lochend and North Roe. Next morning if it was a north-westerly wind one might hear her blow in Westsandwick after she had crossed the sound, and then in Ulsta.

Burravoe had been even more important in days before those I recall, because, as it was her first port of call in Yell, the practice had been to unload there the mails not only for South Yell but for East and Mid Yell, whither they went on by gig. Little time was gained by this arrangement, given the slow progress of a gig on the miserable roads, and it was later decided that the Mid Yell mail should be taken on to Mid Yell by the steamer, but the Burravoe mail continued to be landed at that port whenever the steamer called there. (When she landed mail there on a Sunday evening, people went to the Post Office to collect their letters instead of waiting for them to be delivered on Monday.) Then some bureaucrat came along with the idea that all the mail for Yell was to be landed at Mid Yell, so the steamer was actually supposed to carry the Burravoe mail on instead of landing it at Burravoe. The Burravoe flitmen, with more sense than the officials, persisted in taking the mail ashore and barrowing it up to the Post Office, to be met by a protesting post-mistress, 'I've no authority to accept delivery of the mail'. Officialdom won, with a needless delay in distribution of the local mail. But even so, if one saw or heard the steamer on her way north, then (making allowance for the time it would take her to get to Mid Yell, the time it would take to unload the mail, the time the mail car would take to reach Burravoe and the time it would take the postman to make his rounds) one had a rough idea when to expect the letters. Outgoing mail was altogether more flexible: while the mailboxes were cleared hours before the steamer's departure, often in the previous evening, letters could be handed later to the local merchant, who took them on board when she called on her way south.

The final stage in the delivery of the incoming mail, after it left the local office, has, like most things, undergone changes. 'Johnnie Postie' used to plod on foot from house to house, and indeed any mechanical transport would have been of little help since so many of the houses were a considerable distance from the road and it was much easier to walk from one to the next than to return from each house to the road. Later the postman began to use a push-bike, and then a motor scooter came in, until the extension of side roads, reaching almost every house, made it possible to use a van. These postmen have been a long-serving race: there have been only two in the sixty years I have known Burravoe, each holding office for roughly half of the period.

The *Earl* ceased to call at Burravoe in 1950, on the ground that the flitboat (which had formerly been the Westsandwick flitboat and had replaced a much more handsome vessel at Burravoe) was nearing the end of her life and that there was soon to be a pier at Mid Yell. The withdrawal was, strictly, qualified, for when notice was

L

given it was stated that the steamer would still call for
passengers when required, and the *Earl* did indeed call
occasionally for a few years after 1950, but eventually
even that stopped. The end of the regular, scheduled calls
meant a change in my way of life. I felt, I confess, rather
huffy, and I withdrew my patronage from the steamer for
several years and regularly used the 'overland route' by
bus and ferry instead. I was not entirely a stranger to this
route. My introduction to it was somewhat fortuitous.
When I went north at Easter 1931 and reached Lerwick
after a rather disturbed passage on the *St Catherine,* I
found that Dan Williamson, of Gansons, the car-hirers,
came on board offering to convey passengers to
Mossbank for the ferryboat to Yell. I decided to go, for
this would get me to my destination a good deal sooner
than the *Earl,* which, as she went by Skerries, was not
likely to be in Mid Yell until about 4 p.m. and I would
then have to wait for the mail car to take me to Burravoe.
So I made the 'overland' journey for the first time, left
my suitcase at Ulsta (from which there was no conveyance to Hamnavoe) and Johnnie and I walked over to
Ulsta in the evening to fetch it. In those days it was only
on Wednesdays that there was a regular overland service.
I made a second trip overland in the summer of 1932,
when I wanted to get to Lerwick to meet a friend who was
arriving from Edinburgh and the steamer was not
suitable. On this occasion I got a lift from an
acquaintance who was going back to Lerwick with a
motor bike and sidecar. I have a clearer impression from
this journey of the poor quality of the Mossbank-Lerwick
road, perhaps because the sidecar was more bumpy than
Ganson's bus had been. After these two experiments, I
was never on the overland route again as long as the
steamer could bring me to Burravoe, and it was only after
1950 that I settled for a time into a routine of overland
travel.

The advent of the pier at Mid Yell in 1953 changed

the situation again. It was obviously more comfortable to step on board the steamer at Lerwick and step ashore on a pier at Mid Yell rather than have the chopping and changing — bus, ferry-boat, bus — of the overland service, the chance of getting wet at each change and the possible discomfort of having to stand on the weather side of the ferryboat's deck if there was no room in the cabin. Initially, indeed, the Mid Yell pier was not satisfactory at all states of the tide. On one occasion, when the steamer could not quite reach it, I was transhipped for a few yards in a flitboat and on another, when the steamer could just get her bows up to the pier to work cargo but could not use a gangway, I obeyed a call from the bridge, 'Professor Donaldson, just climb over the fore-heid'. And, of course, there was the need either to wait at Mid Yell for the mail car to take me on to Burravoe or else hire a car. It was not until 1966 that I fully rediscovered the pleasure which the *Earl* afforded and became an addict as never before.

In a sense it was only at this relatively late stage that I began to behave, for the first time, like a tourist. In the spring of 1966 I arranged a trip for myself, as the Company's summer programme of tours had not started. I left Leith on the *St. Ninian* on Monday evening and, with calls at Aberdeen and Kirkwall, arrived at Lerwick late on Wednesday, to spend the night on the ship. Thursday night I was in the Queen's Hotel before joining the *Earl* on the Friday morning. When the whistle of the south boat — the 'old *Clair*', by then the *St. Magnus* (IV), deputising for her successor — woke me, I looked out of my bedroom window over the harbour to see a singularly wintry landscape, covered in snow and with a lowering sky. (I learned by much subsequent experience to expect snow in Shetland in April.) My heart sank as I walked through the snow to board the snow-covered *Earl*, but the snow showers we ran through soon gave way to sunshine. By the time we reached Mid Yell the snow had cleared on land but the *Earl's* foredeck still carried inches of snow and the men on board could snowball those on the pier without fear of retaliation. After a night on board at Baltasound we returned to Lerwick and I went south to Aberdeen.

This whetted my appetite and in September the same year I for the first time booked for one of the Company's inclusive tours. One reason for doing so was that by that time it was known that the days were numbered of the last steamship, the second *St. Clair,* alias *St. Magnus* (IV), and I wanted to make a farewell voyage on her. Keeping in mind how evocative were the sounds of the steamship, I took a tape-recorder with me. I left Leith on Thursday evening for Aberdeen, Kirkwall and Lerwick. At the 12-noon departure from Aberdeen on the Friday I recorded the clatter of the steam-cranes, the three successive bells, the engine-room telegraph, the blast on the whistle, and the cries of the gulls as we moved down the channel. We then had ideal conditions for the passage to Kirkwall, where, so Captain Harvey told me, he rang off at two minutes to ten. On Saturday we had equally fine weather for a trip to Lerwick which was especially memorable. I went up on the bridge immediately I had finished lunch and found Captain Harvey just manoeuvring through the narrow Vasa Sound, anxiously keeping an eye astern to see that the tower of the cathedral was bearing over the west end of Shapinsay. I remarked, 'This is spectacular', to which he replied, 'We've no room to make mistakes'. We went out through Sanday Sound and made for Fair Isle, where we went close in to the east side. Somewhere on the voyage I asked the Captain if he ever went through Mousa Sound now. He said that he hardly ever did so, because the passengers were usually at dinner at that time, but added, somewhat cryptically, 'We could easy do it'. I noted the remark and when I left him to go to the dining saloon as we were approaching Sumburgh I kept it in mind. Fortunately my

seat commanded a view out to the starboard side, where I
wondered if Mousa would in due course appear. When
the southern tip of Mousa did come in sight, I rose from
my coffee, startling my fellow-diners with 'We're going
through Mousa Sound', and dashed up to the bridge with
my camera, exclaiming, 'I'm just in time', to which
Captain Harvey replied, 'It's just as well, for we're doing
it in your honour'.

The arrangement on that tour was to spend Saturday
night on the south boat at Lerwick and transfer to the *Earl*
to spend Sunday night on board before making the round
of the North Isles on the Monday-Tuesday. That was
another trip with a memorable and unexpected episode.
It was the lamb-shipping season, so on the Monday we
pushed on to Baltasound, where we arrived — incredibly
— about 2 p.m., were allowed four hours 'for a run
ashore' as the skipper put it and then left for Brough
Lodge to ship lambs. We arrived off Fetlar to find the
shore brilliantly lit by the evening sunshine. I was briefly
ashore to visit friends and then got back to see the *Earl*
silhouetted against the setting sun, to rejoin her and cross
to Uyeasound, where we lay overnight. On the way south
on Monday there was another special treat, for Captain
Sinclair took the *Earl* close into the waters round the
Horse of Burravoe which I used to know so well in a small
boat.

By this time completely re-converted to 'the
steamer', and increasingly aware that her days were
numbered, I made up my mind never to miss the opportunity of a trip on her. I never went north overland again
until I could go with my own car once a vehicle ferry to
Yell appeared. It became my regular practice to arrive in
Lerwick on a Friday morning, proceed to Mid Yell by the
Earl, have a few days in Yell and then join the *Earl* at Mid
Yell on her northward run on Monday, spend the night
on board at Baltasound and return south on Tuesday. I
arranged if possible to join her on a Monday when she

was due to make her fortnightly call at Hubie, for this offered quite a cruise — from Mid Yell to Cullivoe, Uyeasound, Hubie, Baltasound, Uyeasound, Mid Yell, Skerries, Whalsay and Lerwick, including the run from Hubie to Baltasound by the spectacular and historic east coast of Fetlar, passing Funzie (where some think the Norsemen made their first landing in Shetland), Heilinabretta (scene of the wreck of the 'silver ship' in 1737) and the Brough of strand (with its ancient remains), where I had landed from my own boat in 1935. A degree of unpredictability lingered even to the last years of the North Isles steamer, for although I arranged this trip four times the 'best-laid scheme' was fully carried out only twice. On one occasion there was a south-easter on the Monday, so that the Hubie call had to be postponed until the southward run on Tuesday (between Mid Yell and Skerries) and on another occasion I learned to my dismay that on the Sunday the *Earl* had made an excursion to Hubie and had dealt with her cargo that day, eliminating the need to call on Monday. Even on one of the two occasions when I did get my run from Hubie to Baltasound things did not work our quite as I expected. The *Earl* had a large cargo of coal for Fetlar, all of which had to be transferred to the flitboat in bags and manhandled from the flitboat to the pier, and the laborious process necessitated several journeys for the flitboat and a stay at Hubie of about four hours. I went ashore to visit friends, and the skipper (who had come prepared for what was in store) went ashore with angling tackle to one of the Fetlar lochs. It was a beautiful day, but by the time we were under way for Baltasound the light was beginning to go and I did not see the east side of Fetlar to advantage. On the only one of the four occasions which was completely successful, when Bobby Scott, the steward, came up to the wheelhouse to tell me that tea was ready, I said, 'Thanks, but I can have tea any day. Today I prefer to enjoy the east side of Fetlar.'

I also became an addict of the Mini-Cruises, which offered a trip on the *Earl* as long as she operated. And, as the fatal date of withdrawal came nearer I had a perfect orgy in the spring of 1973, for I followed up the round trip on Friday-Saturday with the round-trip on Monday-Tuesday. By this time I was remarking that my idea of paradise was a season ticket on the North Isles steamer. I was nearly always blessed with fine weather in these last years of the *Earl,* especially going north on Fridays, but it was on one of those two trips in 1973 that I had my solitary experience of missing a port through stress of weather: on the way south on Tuesday, with a tearing nor-wester, we were unable to call at Symbister. I made my last, sad trip, to Whalsay and Hubie, in 1974.

I was often aboard the *Earl* when I was not making a passage on her. It was always possible to go alongside at Burravoe, either in the flitboat or in my own boat, step on board and speak to any passengers I happened to know — and in the holiday season there were sure to be some. I always recall the sense of firmness and stability I felt when my foot came down on the *Earl's* deck as I stepped from a small boat, lively in a restless sea. Each *Earl* had a well-deck forward, around the hatch, for convenience of boat-work, so one stepped right into the midst of the bustle of loading and unloading. For some years it was a regular Saturday morning assignment to be in Burravoe, originally arising from a problem of which the younger generation is quite unaware. Does it ever occur to people now to wonder how a place got the correct time before the days of wireless? The answer is, by the church bell. When the bell of South Yell parish church began to ring at a quarter to twelve on Sunday morning, everyone within earshot checked his clock or watch. But how did the beadle, who rang the bell, get the time? The answer is, from the Post Office. At that time each Post Office received a time signal by telegraph at 10 a.m., and the South Yell beadle, who was my kind host for years, commissioned me to call at the office on Saturday morning and check my watch with the Postmistress. I recall once happening to be in the office at precisely 10 a.m. when the signal came through. Besides getting the time at the Post Office, I also enquired about the steamer, and the postmistress duly 'tinkled' to other offices and informed me, 'She was in Uyeasound at eight o'clock', 'She left Cullivoe at ten' or, 'She left Mid Yell a little ago'. This continued until the telephone came to the North Isles in, I think, 1936. Certainly it was in 1937 that I first *phoned* to Mid Yell to enquire about the steamer.

Of course news that she had left Mid Yell was not an absolute guarantee that Burravoe would ever see her, and over the years she twice failed to turn up. On one occasion, when I was not intending to travel, but merely meant to make my usual social call to see friends on board, a south-easter prevented her from calling. And in 1937, after successive phone calls had brought the news, about 4 p.m., that she had just left Mid Yell, after being held up by fog, we waited, not very optimistically, only to hear her blowing as she went past. I had intended to join her, but it turned out to be a blessing in disguise, for she had to lie fogbound overnight, and the south boat, after waiting until midnight, sailed without her.

The service which the Post Office rendered by giving the time to me and indirectly to the parishioners who set their clocks by the kirk bell, ceased to be necessary with the advent of the wireless set, which was still rare in Yell in the early 1930s. I took an old valve receiver north with me at Christmas 1933, arriving on Christmas Eve. We erected an aerial on the morning of Christmas Day and the first use we made of the set was to listen to King George V addressing the nation at 3 p.m. My hostess remarked very perceptively that his speech was a model of plain, accent-free English; I shudder to think of how she would assess the kind of debased cockney which now habitually assaults our ears from the BBC. Apart from

57   At the Horse of Burravoe

58   From the White Hill to the Horse

59   Lerwick Pier, Saturday evening about 1934

60   Tailpiece: going ashore

giving the time and the news, the wireless was most useful for its weather-forecasts. My boating expeditions never started until after we got the forecast at 10.30 a.m.

8 — 'There's no Place like it'

When I say of Shetland, 'There's no place like it', the sentence has various meanings. It means in the first place the peculiar attraction of familiarity. Time and again in recent years, preparing for a visit to Shetland and even while driving up the road to Aberdeen, I have found myself asking, 'Is it really worth while going to all this bother to revisit territory I have seen times without number and where I shall see nothing I have not seen before?' But as soon as I reach the quay at Aberdeen and board the *St. Clair* the very familiarity of it all captivates me afresh — well-known faces, welcoming hands, the sense already of being a part of a close-knit community. An incident a few years ago exemplifies this. When Captain Thomas Gifford met me on the *St. Clair* (III), he said, 'We've another Burravoe man on board. It's C.D'. Now, I hardly knew C.D., who had lived in Lerwick for years, but I did find him among the passengers and we chatted away. Next morning, as we were going ashore, he asked me what my plans were, and I explained, to which he replied, 'You could have had your breakfast with us'. Now, we were no more than slight acquaintances, but his remark indicated the warmth of a Shetland welcome and the strength of the bonds.

Then the approach to Shetland by sea is something that never palls. How often I have awakened in the morning, I suppose because at that point the ship's motion changed as she came in under the land, to look out and see Sumburgh Head right abeam, lit up by the

rising sun of a summer morning; or in winter to see the
three great flashes of the Sumburgh light, so reassuring in
the darkness — flashes which I have sometimes seen,
reflected against the clouds, from as far away as South
Yell. Over an hour later, when I see yet again the
entrance of Lerwick harbour and the grey town spread
out along the water's edge, I often recall the words of the
Norwegian historian A. W. Brøgger, in his *Ancient
Emigrants:* 'Straight in from the sea, round the Bard Head
and up the fjord of Lerwick, one, in a manner of
speaking, bursts upon Shetland. Shetland: there was
something characteristic about it, from the first moment
we saw it, something peculiarly its own: it was Shetland;
not Norway, not Scotland, but Shetland'. There's no
place like it.

For years and years it was usually a matter, on
arriving in Lerwick, of crossing Victoria Pier and
boarding the North Isles steamer for a voyage to islands
which became progressively more familiar as one
proceeded. Nowadays I more usually drive my car off the
St. Clair at Holmsgarth and head north by land to some of
the more remote areas. And I am at once captivated
afresh by the unique features of the landscape. The rather
shallow soil, with stones protruding through the
vegetation on the hillsides, alternating with deep peat, the
gentle slopes of the hills, the intermingling of land and
sea, the remarkable colouring and the play of sunshine
and shadow. On a May morning, when the mist is just
clearing off and the sun breaks through, some of the
rather bleak growth on the hillsides lights up in a subtle
shade of a kind of subdued pink; or at almost any season
the same thing can happen as the light fades in the
evening, especially on patches of 'lubba' grass.

In May 1981, before I arrived, I had made up my
mind quite firmly that next year I would not make
another visit of the usual type and at the most do a mini-
cruise, but once I was on the road, heading towards

North Roe with a view to exploring the marvellous north-western tip of the Mainland, I felt afresh that Shetland was the one and only place. There is no place like it.

But that sentence has another, less subjective, meaning. It is literally true. I have often remarked, speaking of Orkney, Shetland and Faroe, that they are so different that if one were to be dropped by parachute in any of them one would, given reasonable visibility, know at once in which archipelago one had landed. That may be a hazardous thing to say, bearing in mind Storer Clouston's story *The Man from the Clouds,* where a balloonist who had miscalculated the wind currents thought that he had arrived in North Holland or Germany, 'in some part of the flat wind-swept country not far from the North Sea coast' but found that he was in Orkney. It recalls, too, a story I was told of a boat's crew who went off fishing from Hamnavoe, South Yell. Over-taken by fog, they landed on a shore which was not immediately identifiable, and one of them, something of a know-all, pronounced firmly, 'This is Samphrey'. But when the fog lifted they found they were on the Ness of Galtagarth, in the voe from which they had set out. So I make the qualification, 'given reasonable visibility'.

Seriously, a new appreciation of Shetland came to me when I began to visit other northern lands — not only Orkney, but Faroe, Norway and Iceland — and I discovered that, purely topographically, there is nowhere like Shetland.

Shetland's resemblance to Norway is only a vague one, for the difference of scale is so immense and Shetland has so little that is characteristic of the fjord country of western Norway, where mountains drop into the sea and cultivation and habitation cling precariously to narrow coastal strips or small alluvial areas. The part of the Norwegian coast which most resembles Shetland is in the far north, even beyond the North Cape. Sheer cliffs, fronting the open ocean, dark green hills with burns trickling down the gullies, headlands affording nesting-places to multitudes of birds — these are the typical features. Between the North Cape, which is on the island of Mageroy, and Nordkyn, about fifty miles farther on, which is the most northerly point of the continent of Europe, lies Kjöllefjord, where both the name and the scenery recall Shetland, for there are high cliffs, sometimes broken with patches of grass and sometimes having beaches of shingle at their foot. My comment on Baatsfjord, another port on this stretch of coast, was, 'This is just a Shetland voe, with a village at its head'.

Faroe, while it is strikingly similar to Shetland in having nearly identical land area (about 550 square miles) and a nearly identical length and breadth, has a landscape almost totally different from Shetland. The adjective I always apply to Faroe in my own mind is 'gaunt'. It is as if the corners had never been rubbed off and there is little to soften the scene: the rocks — not patches of rock as in Shetland, but whole seams of rock — break through the hillsides in terraces. The soil is shallow, a lot of the habitation clings rather precariously to the steep hillsides and, while there are some good tracts of meadow-land, Faroe is on the very fringe of the limit for the growth of cereals. Whereas in Orkney there is ample growth of cereals and other crops and even in Shetland there is a modest production of oats and (at least formerly) of barley, in Faroe the thin and scraggy growth of cereals is unrewarding and the preference now is for potatoes. Even in the areas of substantial settlement, the rather bleak mountains are never far away and they are both higher and steeper than anything in Shetland. The Faroese coast, too, seldom tapers off as Shetland's often does, in low-lying nesses with holms and skerries lying off, but the land ends suddenly and drops precipitously into the sea. Precipitously indeed, for neither Orkney nor Shetland nor St. Kilda can offer anything to parallel the Faroese cliffs, which rise to 2500 feet. Faroe has a relatively small number of islands, several of them of comparable size, and this gives the place a different structure from Shetland, where the dominating Mainland provides a kind of unifying backbone for the whole enormous scatter of over 100 islands. The structure of Shetland probably explains why its name is, and always has been, a singular, whereas Orkneyoerne and Faeroerne are plurals, making it correct to speak of 'the Orkneys' or 'the Faroes', whereas 'the Shetlands' is a solecism used only by the ignorant. Resemblances between Faroe and the other island groups can indeed be found here and there. Lerwick and Torshavn each lie approximately one third of the way up the east coast of the archipelago and each stands on the west side of a sound formed by an offshore island: one needs only to look south-east from Torshavn towards the south end of Nolsoy to be struck by the similiarity to the view from Lerwick to Bressay lighthouse. The perpendicular cliffs of Store Dimon are like those of Hoy, and a settlement at Sand, on the Faroese island of Vagar, where 'rigs' descend from the houses to a sandy bay, is not unlike Westsandwick, in Yell.

Orkney stands out among not only the other North Atlantic archipelagos but among all the lands within striking distance of it because of its pre-eminent fertility, which made it a tremendous magnet for settlers and endowed it with its unparalleled prehistoric and historic monuments, evidence of a prosperous and flourishing culture extending over millennia. The character of the Orkney landscape is changing all the time as one proceeds from the south-west to the north-east. Hoy is almost mountainous, reaching over 1500 feet, but nowhere else is there a hill exceeding 800 feet; nor are there cliffs anywhere else which come near to matching Hoy's. The contrast between Hoy and the lower profile of the rest of Orkney is the more marked because its massive bulk is visible from so many areas. Most of the other islands are at best undulating, but when we reach the North Isles we come on pieces of land almost as flat as pancakes. One does not need to be far off Sanday and North Ronaldsay for these islands to become mere lines on the horizon, and they forcibly recall the Dutch coast, for the land soon vanishes from sight, leaving a few conspicuous buildings still visible above the horizon. The Scottish island they most resemble is Tiree. On a bad day, with a sea running, hardly anything can be seen of North Ronaldsay except the lighthouse tower. Some of Orkney is best seen from the air, when its well cultivated fields are so clear, but the slopes of its low hills, capable of being cultivated almost if not quite to their summits, form what I mentally call a smiling landscape. There is no mistaking Shetland cliffs for Orkney cliffs, because of the different composition of the rocks and the different planes of the strata. One or two exceptionally fertile areas in Shetland approximate to what one finds in Orkney — parts of Dunrossness, for example, and around Aith. But generally in Shetland the arable areas are mere fringes round great tracts of moor and hill, and the whole landscape is rougher. The intermingling of land and water is more fantastic in Shetland, with its deeply-indented coast, than in Orkney and, despite the stretches of cliff-girt coast, often dropping steeply into the sea, a good deal of the Shetland coastline consists of land sloping rather gradually into the sea, with holms and skerries lying off and taking away something of the starkness. Except when seen on very dull, dark or stormy days, the Shetland landscape is not unkindly looking, but it seldom smiles in just the way that Orkney smiles.

Because these northern lands are so different one from another, each has its attractions and its devotees and he would be an insensitive man who could not write appreciatively of all of them, even although his own preferences must lie with the land where there is a happy memory at every corner. Part of the charm of the

Shetland landscape undoubtedly arises from its perfection of scale: it has almost everything, but all in the proportions of a miniature. The vast expanses of the Scottish Highlands, or the even vaster expanses of Norway, can stand mountains of 4000 feet and more, but any such peak in Shetland would be quite out of place. Much of the coastal scenery is splendid, it is grand, but except when viewed, as it ought to be, from a small boat, it is seldom startling. The one exception perhaps is the Kame of Foula, rearing its 1220 feet out of the sea and up from the surface of an island only about three miles in diameter. Other cliffs, though they rise to over 900 feet at Fitful Head and not much less at Saxavord, blend into the general pattern, the general proportions. Equally, the great expanses in inland scenery hardly ever stretch far enough to become tedious, and any pieces of country which could be called uninteresting hardly ever last long enough to be tiresome, even for a pedestrian. I suppose the Lang Kames on the road between Lerwick and the north Mainland are an exception, but now that there is such a superb road through them the question of tedium hardly arises, at any rate to a motorist. It must have been a melancholy enough route in the days when my father's uncle walked from Mossbank to Lerwick. The adjoining Kergord-Weisdale area has a totally different character from any other part of Shetland, because not only is it a very broad valley but because the massive but rounded hills are green almost if not quite to their summits, and this, in conjunction with the not inconsiderable plantation of trees, far superior many of them to the stunted specimens found elsewhere in Shetland, helps to give the place its character. It is perhaps the one part of Shetland which one might mistake for Lowland Scotland and where one could easily be in the Border hills. If one proceeds from Weisdale on to the road which runs west to Sandwater to join the main route to the north, one finds there again a broad valley but the hills now are

thoroughly peaty, there is no greenery, there are no trees
and the whole effect becomes much more typical of
Shetland and much more desolate.

It was not only in respect of the landscape that a new
appreciation of Shetland came to me after I began to visit
other northern lands. There were similarities as well as
differences among them in the way of life and in material
culture. Shetland must be seen in its setting as centrally
placed in an ancient cultural area, where much the same
race, language and way of life at one time prevailed. I
have sometimes asked, 'What do they know of Shetland
who only Shetland know?'

Place-names furnish one of the strongest visible and
audible links between Shetland and the other northern
countries, and one of the strongest living proofs that a
thousand years ago there was a unity extending over
hundreds of miles of northern ocean. This has remained
true despite the efforts of Scottish map-makers to obscure
or obliterate the native forms. Readers of this book may
have noticed some spellings of place-names which they
will not find on the map. But, as intelligent observers,
even if not versed in etymology, have long realised, it is
the maps that are wrong. A hundred years ago Tudor
noticed that the map was studded with absurd spellings
and tried to rectify some of them. He preferred Rooeness
and Muckle Rooe to other spellings, and remarked that
' "Ronas Hill" is nonsense'. He also gave the correct
'Wais' or 'Waas' as alternatives to the false 'Walls', and
preferred 'Haraldswick' to 'Haroldswick'. Although he
realised the tautology involved in usages like 'Laxfirth
Voe', he adhered in the main to the 'firth' form, which
represents neither local pronunciation nor Norse origins,
but he courageously achieved 'Burra Fiord'. A gallant
attempt to put things right was made in Manson's *Guide to
Shetland* in the 1930s, but by that time it was far too late. I
may find difficulty between reproducing falsehood and
mystifying my readers, but I flatly refuse to use, for
example, 'Whale Firth'.

M

Place-names are peculiarly enduring, are almost impervious to political, social and even some linguistic changes, and to this day they are in Shetland nearly 100% Norse. My acquaintance with the meaning of the elements in Shetland place-names has sometimes helped me to understand a Danish or Norwegian word, perhaps in a notice, and in Iceland, where the language has continued with little change, you will still see and hear the very syllables which went to form a place-name in Shetland a thousand years ago. Many Shetland names are still easily recognisable as identical with names in other northern lands: e.g., Collafirth in Shetland, Kjöllefjord in the north of Norway and Kollafjord in Faroe; and the classic example of Tingwall in Shetland and in Orkney, Thingvellir in Iceland, Dingwall in Scotland and Tynwald in the Isle of Man. The similarities between Shetland and the Faroes are peculiarly striking and much closer than any between Shetland and Orkney. The southmost point of Faroe, if we except some rocks, is Sumbo, which seems to have been copied from Sumburgh; there is Haraldsund between two of the most northerly islands of Faroe, like Haraldswick in Unst; the longest voe in Faroe used to be called Solmundarfjord, as the longest voe in Shetland is Sullom Voe; Skallevik is parallel to Scalloway; and one comes on Saltnes, Kaldbaksnes, Hvitanes (= Whiteness), Leirvik and many more.

As one travels around the northern countries and meets a familiar name in a strange land, one often has a curious sense of belonging, a sense almost of coming home. For example, in the course of two successive summers I visited a place in the far north of Norway called Melbu, I spent a couple of nights in a place in Shetland called Melby and I spent a couple of nights in a place in Denmark called Magleby (pronounced Mailboo), all of which I take to be the same. The most striking example in my experience was this: as readers of chapters

3 and 4 must have learned, there were few places I saw more frequently than the little Shetland island of Orfasay; and when I was entering the harbour of Reykjavik in Iceland for the first time I happened to be talking to an Icelander, who pointed to a little island and remarked, 'That's Irfirso'. Even before I visited Norway I learned how this experience could arise, when on the stern of a Bergen-registered ship lying at Granton I saw the name 'Blaafiel', the name of a hill in South Yell.

All of those place-names have their meanings, sometimes at once obvious, like Hamnavoe (= haven voe or sheltered voe), Roe (= the red island), Laxfirth (= salmon firth), sometimes not too obvious. On some of the more cryptic I have often turned to Professor Herman Palsson for enlightenment: that peculiar curved spit of shingle which projects into Westsandwick Voe, the Urra Bug, he pronounced to mean 'the hard bow', and Hascosay, I learned, means 'sea-wood isle', I suppose because it was a good place for gathering driftwood cast up by a south-easter. But Orfasay/Irfirso raises a point of interest. The name signifies a tidal island, and is cognate with Oronsay in the Hebrides. But the Shetland Orfasay is not and never was a tidal island: the *Earl* used to go through Orfasay Sound. And this raises the question whether a name which, like others, is ostensibly descriptive, may fail to describe accurately the place to which it is applied, because it was introduced by immigrants and transferred from a place they knew at home rather than conferred of new on a place where they settled. The close parallels between Shetland and Faroe, mentioned above, might well be the result of migration from one group of islands to the other and the transference of names. There is the case of Borgarfjordur in Iceland. The identical Burrafirth in Shetland signifies a feature with a broch nearby, as do Burravoe and Burraness. But as there were no brochs in Iceland, the question arises whether Borgarfjordur was taken to

Iceland by immigrants. There must be many doubtful cases. For example, 'the bird island' could be expected to be a very common descriptive name, and it does occur several times. But Fuglöy in the north of Norway, Fugloy in the north of Faroe and Foula in Shetland all have marked points of resemblance, especially in the conspicuous feature of presenting a great bastion of cliffs to the open ocean. Now, is the name always essentially descriptive, or did migrants from one of those places take the name with them and give it to an island resembling one they had known at home? This occurred to me as I recalled a very fine sunset behind Foula in Shetland when I was watching the sun go down — I cannot say 'set', because it did not go completely below the horizon at midnight — behind Fuglöy in northern Norway. Place-name students have to use their eyes as well as their ears.

The place-names of Shetland are a precious possession, unchanged not just for sixty years, but for a thousand years, and peculiarly evocative. Everything should be done to retain them and foster their use. I was struck by the contrast between Shetland and Argyll in respect of place-name survival. In Shetland, while I have no doubt many names have fallen and are falling out of use, there is still a great wealth of them on everyone's lips. In the West Highlands, the names of physical features seem to be dropping out of use more and more and only the names of habitations are retained. The contrast was impressed on me in my boating experience. In Shetland I never had any difficulty in explaining where I had been or where I had seen something: it would be at the Corbie Gios or the Point of Capel or the Windy Clett or the Burgi Skerries. But in Argyll, where no one uses the names of coastal features, I was driven to some circumlocution: it was 'the point beyond the Tower' or 'the second point' or 'the bay where the salmon fisherman has his hut' or something of that kind. Very frustrating. The real name of a bay will disappear, and instead it will be named after the farm at its head. When one of the older inhabitants did use the proper name of a rock or a point he did it with a smile, as if he did not expect to be taken seriously. Part of the explanation of this may be that the place-names in the West Highlands are of course Gaelic, which is still a living language for a number of people, with the result that if someone knows Gaelic he is apt to translate a place-name into English. You will find Eilean Dubh on the map, but everyone calls it 'The Black Isle'. That is detrimental to the stability of place-names. In Shetland, the language from which the place-names derive is a dead language and indeed the place-names may be used without knowledge of their meaning. So we have Swarta Skerry and not 'The Black Rock'. This, I believe, helps to preserve the place-names in everyday use.

No opportunity should be lost to discourage the tendency of some individuals and some local authorities to disregard local place-name tradition. True, some 'foreign' names of one kind or another were introduced a long time ago and have been made respectable by antiquity. Belmont in Unst, I suppose, may be an example, or Smithfield in Fetlar. And Altona in Mid Yell, which, I have been told, occurs at least as far back as about 1800, might perhaps have been introduced by a merchant from Hamburg, which the original Altona adjoins. But in recent years the authorities, in Shetland as elsewhere, have been almost incredibly insensitive on this issue. A bad example was set by the central government when it insisted on giving the name Glenrothes to a new town which is not in a glen and is about a hundred miles from Rothes. 'Morven View' was once proposed for a housing scheme in Fort William by Inverness-shire County Council, but the Town Council very properly turned it down. In Shetland there have been monstrosities like 'Carlton Terrace', but of late more sense has sometimes been shown. My experience in Argyll showed that private enterprise could make a modest contribution to the preservation of the place-name heritage. The County Council would have called some new houses in North Connel 'Loch Nell View' (which was wrong anyway, because the stretch of water they looked out on was Ardmucknish Bay and not Loch Nell), but the matter was referred to the District Council, and the local District Councillor, who was my neighbour, consulted me. I proposed the Gaelic for 'the field of the ferry' — Dal-an-aiseig — because the site was adjacent to the old ferry pier at the mouth of Loch Etive, and this was accepted. I called my own two successive houses Altnavullin (the Burn of the Mill — but here, in my imperfect knowledge of Gaelic, I made a grammatical error) and Camallt (the Winding Burn), and I obliged other proprietors of new houses with Craigavullin (the Rock of the Mill) and Tigh-n-Drochaid (the House of the Bridge). No doubt these names are now in the Valuation Roll if not on the map, and one wonders if a place-name scholar in the future will realise that they were bestowed so recently as the 1960s.

Sometimes the Norse element in modern Shetland speech has been exaggerated, for the dialect is fundamentally derived from *old* Lowland Scots, and some of the words believed to be of Norse origin are to be found in old Scots as well. 'Grice' meaning a pig is both Scots and Norse, but remains in more common use in Shetland, where 'a lazy grice' is a term of abuse and there is a riddle about 'twa grey grice lying in a sty' to which the answer is 'two millstones'. 'Gate' meaning a road or path is another example, and it perhaps owes its survival in Shetland to the fact that Shetlanders still use 'grind' for 'gate'. On the other hand, some Shetland terms believed to be modifications of Scots or English are really Norse. The Shetlander's 'enoo', which is readily taken to be a version of the English 'even now', is pure Norse — 'endnu' in modern Danish. I realised this when, in Denmark, I rose to leave a bus too soon and a lady checked me, 'Ikke endnu' — 'Not yet' — pronouncing 'endnu' exactly as a Shetlander pronounces 'enoo'. When a Shetlander speaks of a 'burden' of say, hay, is he really using the English 'burden' or the Norse 'byrdi', still current in Iceland with the same meaning? When a Shetlander uses 'follow' in the sense of accompany, he accords with Scandinavian usage, where one verb has both meanings; so with 'lock' meaning to close a door (for 'key' is used as a verb); and the use of 'first' as 'in the first of the year' or 'in the first of May', where a Dane would say 'fØrst i Maj'. Even 'learn' meaning 'teach' — though that is a Scotticism — finds justification in Danish, where 'laere' is used in both senses (as indeed 'lehren' is in German). Usages which seem to have arisen from a misunderstanding of English are (probably) 'traivel' meaning to walk, 'annoyed' meaning worried or anxious and 'clever' meaning quick. One of the most tenacious usages to survive amid a mixture of old Scots with Norse words and idioms is the second person singular 'du', like the French 'tu' and the German 'du'. I recall once a Shetland home where there was a very young child who regarded me as a stranger and remarked in a shocked tone, 'Mammy said "du" to Gordon'.

The peoples who speak the various languages which derive in whole or in part from the Norse of a thousand years ago have certain characteristics in their persons which point to a common racial origin too. The idea that the northern lands are inhabited by fair-haired, blue-eyed giants is quite wrong, or at least a gross exaggeration. There is a dark strain everywhere, and it is not at all clear that it is due only, or even mainly, to immigration from southern lands. In Norway, the people become perceptibly darker as you go farther north, owing possibly to the intermingling of the blood of the Lapps, who preserve their own society and culture in the far north, but that is only part of the explanation. In Iceland, the two distinct fair and dark strains are quite conspicuous, and, while it is possible that the dark strain owes something to pre-Norse settlers, perhaps from Ireland, it must be seen in the context of the varied physical characteristics visible in the Scandinavia from which most Icelanders came. The Faroes, too, have plenty of dark people. There may quite possibly have been a pre-Norse migration from Scandinavia to the Atlantic islands, a migration of a short, dark race — the semi-legendary Finns, perhaps — who found their way to various parts of the north. So when in Shetland one sees the many dark people — some of them very dark — there is no need to think that they are descended from ship-wrecked sailors off the Spanish Armada. They may have an ancestry going back to pre-Norse settlers or to the dark strain which came in with the Scandinavian settlers themselves. I have sometimes noticed very striking resemblances between dark Shetlanders whom I know and men I have seen in Faroe or Iceland. When Tudor remarked of Shetlanders that they generally have a 'viking' appearance, it is hard to know what he meant. If he meant that they are predominantly tall, fair-haired and blue-eyed, he was wrong, but his remark was not necessarily wide of the mark. Curiously enough, he rightly drew attention to the singular beauty of many Shetland women, and he must have noticed that the most characteristic Shetland female type is a dark type.

As in language and race, so in material culture, one does not go far to see reflections of the ancient connection among the northern lands. This is not very noticeable in buildings. The Norsemen took with them their habit of building in wood from their homeland where timber was abundant to treeless areas like Faroe and Iceland, to which almost every scrap of wood had to be imported, and in those areas it has persisted (though recently run-concrete has tended to prevail). It must surely be assumed that the tradition of building in wood came to Shetland too, and Mr Brian Smith has recently brought together significant evidence to this effect. Yet in Shetland the buildings have long been predominantly of stone, presumably because new building techniques were brought in by the many Scottish immigrants. It seems, too, that the borrowing was from Lowland Scotland, where corners were squared off, and not from the Highlands, where the houses had rounded corners. It is true that in Faroe there are some houses built largely of stone, but they are of quite a different character from those in Shetland.

The wooden buildings of the north lend themselves to colour. In contrast to our drab greys and blacks, villages and towns everywhere else are a blaze of colour, particularly green and red, in addition to white, with the result that even on a dull day a place looks bright and cheerful. The disadvantage of course is that wood de-teriorates rapidly unless it is maintained, and in towns like Torshavn and Reykjavik there were some perfectly appalling tumble-down shacks, perhaps paralleled in Shetland only in the shanty-town of the old North Road in Lerwick. The other thing that one misses with wooden buildings is the existence of structures of any great antiquity. The oldest building in Iceland, a church, dates from only about 1800. The same applies very largely to Faroe, though there is a concentration of older houses at Tinganes and there is the remarkable exception of the unfinished stone cathedral at Kirkjubo. In Norway there are a few stone churches of great age, and the remarkable wooden stave-churches which go back to early medieval times, but the churches of later date are predominantly of wood except for a few in the large towns. It is only in Denmark that one reaches a land where buildings were long ago of stone or brick and where almost every village has a church going back at least in part to the twelfth century or so. Shetland has the remains of quite a number of medieval stone churches, and this perhaps raises a question whether wooden houses can ever have been general.

One building feature common to the northern lands is the turf roof, which is still familiar in Shetland on outhouses. But the 'fealy roof' of a Shetland outhouse is a humble affair compared with the turf roofs elsewhere. The turf that is put on seems to be thicker, so that it bears grass more readily, and the grass grows so abundantly that it can be — and sometimes is — grazed by sheep or mown with a scythe. The effect is very picturesque and really rather tidy. Even large modern buildings, like a hospital near Torshavn, have been roofed in this way. Possibly the fondness for painting wooden roofs green derives from the green roofs of turf.

The ancient unity of culture is reflected less in buildings than it is in implements and artefacts, which are often almost identical. The old-fashioned plunger churn, which remained so popular in Shetland as long as churning prevailed that one seldom saw any other kind of 'kirn' in use, was as widely used in Norway and Iceland, and models of it are common souvenirs in all three lands. Shetland and Faroese spades, Shetland and Faroese 'klibbers' (used for attaching panniers to ponies' backs) are very similar. Then there is the bailer or 'auskerry' for use in a boat. A Shetland example, made of wood, is closely parallel to Faroese and Norwegian models, and it is now possible to buy, in a ship-chandler's in Bergen, a plastic product which does not vary from the traditional and well-tried design.

These words, 'traditional and well-tried design', apply with special force to what is perhaps the most conspicuous product of human craftsmanship which takes much the same form in all the northern lands, namely the boat. We may suppose that more than a thousand years ago an unknown genius in Norway devised a shape of hull and a method of construction of superlative sea-worthiness and possessed of many other advantages. In all the centuries since, it has not been found possible to improve on that ancient design in essentials, and very much the same type of boat persists to this day in most of the regions of Scandinavian settlement, with only minor local variants which give their own character to the boats of Norway, Shetland, Orkney, Faroe and Iceland. There is still no doubt that Shetlanders' thoughts are never far from the sea which surrounds them and that their boats have a high place in their affections. All round the shores are to be seen plenty of boats, usually showing all the signs of loving care. The majority of them are still of the classic Shetland model, whose lines are such a delight to the eye that one can look for minutes on end simply appreciating the wonderful design which has come down to us over the centuries. When I lecture on the Scandinavian factor in Scottish history I always show a series of pictures of boats in the different northern countries, to indicate the general similarity and the major variants. When I had a Shetland boat in the West Highlands, I was twice asked (by people fairly knowledgeable about boats), 'Is that a Swedish boat you've got?' They at once recognised the boat as belonging to the northern family, as it were, and as being foreign to Scotland. More striking was an incident when I was putting together the illustrations for *Shetland Life under Earl Patrick*. I had photographs of a group of boats drawn up on a beach in Iceland and of another group of boats in rather similar formation on the beach at the Manor House in Burravoe, and handed them in with others to the block-maker. I called a few days later to ask how the work was getting on, and the block-maker said, 'Of course we didn't make blocks of both of those, because they are so much alike that it didn't seem worth while to have them both'. Which was exactly what I wanted to prove.

Until a few years ago it was rare to see a square-sterned boat or anything other than a Shetland model, but now moulded hulls of various types, usually powered by outboard motors, mainly heavy, have become relatively common. In this Shetland is following Norway,

where the local boats seem now to be in a minority, and it
is to be hoped that the traditional Shetland boat, with its
superb buoyancy and its many practical advantages for
Shetland beaches and Shetland waters, as well as its grace
of lines, will continue to have a place in the life of the
community and to recall that Shetland belonged to a far-
flung culture extending from the Baltic to the Greenland
settlements and from the North Cape to the Isle of Man.